"Everything Phil Callaway writes is full of life because he's discovered a fabulous secret: The joy of Christ doesn't go away, even when life is a mess."

LUIS PALAU
International evangelist
author of *God is Relevant*

"Very likely Phil Callaway has the best sense of humor in the Western hemisphere. One page into this book and I'm quaking with laughter. Callaway has the uncanny ability to uncover the funny in any situation and report it with inspirational wit. In these pages, however, he faces the ultimate test: Can he quarry humor from the rock-hard reverses and tragedies of life? Read on: Like me, you'll be pleasantly surprised!"

PAUL L. MAIER
Author of *A Skeleton In God's Closet*

"Life's tough lessons are so much easier to handle if you can do it with a chuckle. In no way does that minimize the struggle of the hard times. They are real. They are painful. And we all have our share. But God has given us a sense of humor as one of our defenses against despair. Thankfully Phil really knows how to get in touch with his spiritual funnybone."

JANETTE OKE
Bestselling author

"Life's funny. Just when you think everything's coming up roses, you find a skunk running loose in your garden. Phil Callaway has had to deal with his share of life's skunks, but in his gifted, witty way, he reminds us of where we need to be placing our focus. This book is an excellent source of encouragement for anyone in the midst of a crisis who may be asking God that hardest question of all: 'Why?'"

MARTHA BOLTON
Bob Hope staff writer, author, director of Glasgow Comedy College

"Don't buy a copy of this book. Buy a few dozen. Phil's formula for skunkbusting sparkles. His stories of hope and laughter shine. These paragraphs are loaded pistols; the conclusions are dynamite. If this book doesn't make you chuckle until you cry, you'd better ask your doctor to operate on your funnybone."

JOEL FREEMAN
Author of *God Is Not Fair,* chaplain of the NBA's Washington Wizards

"Phil Callaway's books are like ice cream cones. You want to savor the whole thing, go back for more, and share a lick or two with the ones you love. Go ahead. Enjoy yourself. These stories are good for your soul."

CHRIS FABRY
Broadcaster, author of *At the Corner of Mundane and Grace*

"With humor and pathos, Phil Callaway proves once again that his heart is in the right place. You'll find *Who Put the Skunk in the Trunk?* A fascinating and heartwarming read."

MIKE YORKEY
Author of *Touched by the Savior,* former editor of *Focus on the Family* magazine

"Phil Callaway loves to write in a lighthearted, humorous way about everyday events common to us all. In this book, however, his humor faces the challenge of real tragedy. The intersection results in a deepening understanding of God and a life still graced by laughter. A recommended read for all of us whose faith has been challenged by bad times beyond our control."

JOHN FISCHER
Author of *Ashes on the Wind* and *12 steps for the Recovering Pharisee*

"I love Phil Callaway because he manages to accomplish what few writers can—masterfully blending laughter with learning. Read this book and you'll experience both!"

LEE STROBEL
Author of *The Case for Christ*

"I can't think of a better way to get rid of the skunks in your life and redirect your thoughts back to our Lord, the source of Joy."

LARRY BURKETT
Author, founder and CEO, Christian Financial Concepts

Who put the Skunk in the Trunk?

LEARNING TO LAUGH WHEN LIFE STINKS

PHIL CALLAWAY

Multnomah®Publishers *Sisters, Oregon*

WHO PUT THE SKUNK IN THE TRUNK?
published by Multnomah Publishers, Inc.

© 1999 by Phil Callaway
International Standard Book Number: 1-57673-576-1

Cover illustration by Gary Ciccarelli
Design by Stephen Gardner

Scripture quotations are from:
Holy Bible, New Living Translation © 1996. Used by permission of
Tyndale House Publishers, Inc. All rights reserved.

Also quoted:
The Holy Bible, New International Version (NIV)
© 1973, 1984 by International Bible Society,
used by permission of Zondervan Publishing House.

Cartoon on pages 65, 144, 156, 194 taken from "Motherhood is
Stranger Than Fiction" by Mary Chambers. © 1995 Mary Chambers.
Used by permission of InterVarsity Press.

Cartoons on pages 28, 45, 59, 91, 99, 108, 184 by John McPherson.

Multnomah is a trademark of Multnomah Publishers, Inc.,
and is registered in the U.S. Patent and Trademark Office.
The colophon is a trademark of Multnomah Publishers, Inc.

Printed in the United States of America

For information:
MULTNOMAH PUBLISHERS, INC.
POST OFFICE BOX 1720
SISTERS, OREGON 97759

Library of Congress Cataloging-in-Publication Data:
Callaway, Phil, 1961– Who put the skunk in the trunk?: learning to
laugh when life stinks/by Phil Callaway. p.cm.
ISBN 1-57673-576-1 (alk. paper) 1. Christian life Anecdotes.
2. Callaway, Phil, 1961– I. Title
BV4517.C34   1999   242–dc21   99-40423   CIP

99 00 01 02 03 04 — 10 9 8 7 6 5 4 3 2 1

FOR RAMONA

The apple in my pie.
The glue in my marriage.
The girl of my dreams.
If I knew it would have been this good…
I'd have asked you to marry me in sixth grade.

Special Delivery. . .

After fathering three children and authoring five books, I now feel qualified to say something insightful. I believe that the closest a man will ever come to giving birth is writing a book. During the past nine months, this "baby" has been ever before me. I have not always been rational. I sometimes snack late at night. I once ate a full jar of dill pickles. And was sick in the morning. The book you now hold (weighing in at thirteen ounces) was conceived about seventy-seven months ago as life began to take some strange twists for me and my wife. As with any project this monumental, it would not have been accomplished without the nourishment, coaching, and support of people like the pizza delivery guy.

I would also like to thank my wife Ramona, who kept saying, "Honey, breathe deeply. You know, like you told me in the delivery room just before you passed out." I am also deeply grateful to Jeffrey, Rachael, and Stephen, three wonderful children who hang around our house, sometimes encouraging me to procrastinate by saying, "Dad, how about we bring that pizza to the living room and watch Ben Hur, The Great Escape, and The Ten Commandments?"

Thanks to more than forty couples who keep me in their prayers. And to Mom and Dad who talk more about me on their knees than anywhere else. Hats off to my family of friends at Prairie Bible Institute, particularly Dan and Lynn, Tim and Ruth, Vance and Sherri, James and Anne, and Ahab and Jezebel—two Labrador retrievers I walk past each day. They help me get to work on time.

Philip Yancey, Gloria Gaither, Joni Eareckson Tada, Elizabeth Elliot, Barbara Johnson, and Twila Paris provided wonderful answers to my questions. Jon Detweiler, a good friend, allowed me to plagiarize a few of his paragraphs. Canadian Airlines provided numerous delays so I could complete entire chapters in fine airports everywhere. Other corporate sponsors: Lego kept my children busy while I wrote, the Coffee Break provided delicious reasons to be out to lunch, and Coca-Cola kept me awake.

If you've ever seen a turtle on a fence post, you know that he had to have help getting there, so I'd like to thank the fine folks at Multnomah for the lift. They nurtured this baby from day one, taking regular ultrasounds and commenting often, "Hey, I think that's a chapter there. I can see it moving." David Van Diest spent $6.85 on lunch for me in Denver (a fish filet sandwich) and landed this book (next time I'll go with the steak and triple-fudge sundae). Cliff Boersma provided invaluable counsel, as well as a nice advance. Nancy Thompson talked softly and carried a big eraser. And Steve Gardner, a very wise art director, agreed not to put a cartoon of me on the cover. Thanks, guys, for putting me on this post.

Most of all, I thank God for entrusting me with a most precious gift. The gift of laughter. I would be building birdhouses in a home for the bewildered were it not for this gift. To think that I now make a living doing something I got the strap for throughout elementary school (helping people laugh) is downright astounding. Thank you Lord for taking a hardened hypocrite, turning me upside-down, and somehow using me. May everything I write show my thankful heart.

Finally, a great big thanks to you the reader. Your time is precious. I pledge not to waste it. Your letters of encouragement over the years were more than enough to coax me back to the delivery room one more time. Thanks for picking this baby up. I hope it behaves quite nicely.

Contents

INTRODUCTION: *Hey Honey, That's Us—Les Misérables!* 11

SKUNKBUSTER SECRET #1:
The World Is Full of Cactus...but You Don't Have to Sit on One 16

CHAPTER ONE:
Who Put the Skunk in the Trunk? 17

CHAPTER TWO:
Stuff Happens 23

CHAPTER THREE:
What about Bob? 29

CHAPTER FOUR:
Lessons on Ice 35

CHAPTER FIVE:
The Choice 41

CHAPTER SIX:
I Broke My Leg Today...At Least It Wasn't My Neck 47

CHAPTER SEVEN:
The Envelope, Please 53

SKUNKBUSTER SECRET #2:
When Opportunity Knocks, Don't Complain about the Noise 60

CHAPTER EIGHT:
Help! We're Breaking Out in Toddlers! 61

CHAPTER NINE:
The Last Shoe Box 67

CHAPTER TEN:
Reluctant Hero 73

CHAPTER ELEVEN:
The Long Good-Bye 79

CHAPTER TWELVE:
Dreams on Ice 85

CHAPTER THIRTEEN:
Laughter in the Valley 93

SKUNKBUSTER SECRET #3:
Courage Is Fear That Has Said Its Prayers 100

CHAPTER FOURTEEN:
Daddy Is Awake 101

CHAPTER FIFTEEN:
Journey into Trust 109

Contents

CHAPTER SIXTEEN:
A Wing and a Bet 117

CHAPTER SEVENTEEN:
A Tale of Two Kings 121

CHAPTER EIGHTEEN:
Hey! Look Who Won the Rat Race! 127

CHAPTER NINETEEN:
The Stuttering Servant 133

CHAPTER TWENTY:
Commencement Address to the Class of '99 139

SKUNKBUSTER SECRET #4:
Laughter Is Ice Cream on the Pie of Life.
It Adds Flavor and Makes It Easier to Swallow. 146

CHAPTER TWENTY-ONE:
Laughter 101 147

CHAPTER TWENTY-TWO:
Who Put the Frog in My Peas? 157

CHAPTER TWENTY-THREE:
Letter in a Lunch Box 165

CHAPTER TWENTY-FOUR:
Celebrity Skunks 171

SKUNKBUSTER SECRET #5:
Laughter Sure Beats Prozac, but There's No Medicine Quite Like Hope. 180

CHAPTER TWENTY-FIVE:
Tales of Mischief 181

CHAPTER TWENTY-SIX:
The Gospel According to Matt 185

CHAPTER TWENTY-SEVEN:
Why Methuselah Lived So Long 191

CHAPTER TWENTY-EIGHT:
The Last Resort 195

CHAPTER TWENTY-NINE:
Hope for Christmas 203

CHAPTER THIRTY:
A Place Called Home 211

EPILOGUE 215

Hey Honey, That's Us— Les Miserables!

"Everything is funny as long as it is happening to somebody else."
WILL ROGERS

I t was the best of days. It was the worst of days.
Friday, August 28, 1992.
Our tenth anniversary.

A week earlier I had called the Delta Bow Valley Hotel to reserve room 1716. The manager asked why in the world I wanted that particular room, so I told him: "Our irish setter had a fine litter of pups on that bed, so we're bringing the Saint Bernard this time."

Thankfully he laughed.

"Actually," I said, with a smile in my voice, "we got our marriage off to a great start in that room, and we'd like to return every ten years or so if you'll let us." He assured me that he would, and furthermore, there would be a few surprises waiting when we arrived. The first surprise was that the room would now cost

$119, inflated slightly from the $39 we had paid ten years ago. I hung up the phone, then called for tickets to *Les Misérables,* a famous opera which millions have seen but no one can properly pronounce.

"I need a credit card number," said the ticket agent.

"How much will it cost?" I asked, pulling a well-worn VISA card from my wallet.

"Seventy dollars."

I instinctively clutched my billfold. "Um…is that per row?"

"That is per seat, sir," said he, without the slightest trace of humor.

Two hundred and fifty-nine dollars later I had the perfect romantic getaway planned. A whole twenty-four hours to celebrate a love which had begun to blossom fifteen years earlier when a shy blonde from a thousand miles away moved in next door, causing me to claim Galatians 5:14 as my high school motto:

The whole law can be summed up in this one command:
"Love your neighbor as yourself."

We dated on and off for five years (off whenever she said so) and on a rainy day in August, tied the knot. Ten years later, we had three wonderful children and a marriage filled with more joy than either of us could have imagined. But as I put away my VISA card that day, I realized that much of the joy had faded.

Would the weekend help us forget the dark clouds that had begun hovering over us five months earlier?

I wondered.

In March of that year, events had taken place that neither us nor a dozen doctors could explain. Events that had forced us to our knees and sometimes to despair. In my book *Making Life Rich Without Any Money* (Harvest House), I tell the story of the wintry day when I came home to discover our five-, three- , and two-year-olds alone in the kitchen trying to create their own breakfast.

Looking up at me with frightened eyes, our eldest son Stephen asked, "Is Momma gonna die?"

In the living room, Ramona lay unconscious in a pool of blood, an ugly gash running down her leg. She had just experienced the first seizure of her life. The first of hundreds to come.

During the long ambulance ride to a nearby city, I wondered what the future held. Until now, my life had been smooth sailing. Pain was something that invaded other people's lives. I had easy answers to their questions. I could spout clichés with the best of them. But today as I looked down on the only girl I'd ever fallen for, I knew my world was about to change. Yesterday Ramona was so full of life, her welcome-home kiss delivered with the sweetest of smiles, her face bright with laughter. Today she lay close to death, her lips a dark blue, her pretty face a pale shade of gray. Holding her motionless hand, I stared out the window, tears streaming down my face. "Oh God," I prayed, "if you're really there, please do something."

But God didn't seem to hear.

The next few months brought with them an endless procession of doctors, specialists, hospital rooms, and the frustration of living every waking moment with a sword dangling over our heads. The seizures worsened. By August we had resigned ourselves to the fact that the only certain thing about our new life was that it would be filled with uncertainty. Anxious days and sleepless nights drained the laughter from our lives and caused me to welcome a new and unpleasant guest into our home. On the outside I seemed resilient. Strong. Even joyful. But inside bitterness began to haunt me like a West Coast rain that won't lift.

The anniversary weekend was our first weekend alone since March, and I'd been looking forward to it for weeks. Perhaps the rain would lighten up for a few days. Maybe even the sun would shine.

Pulling into the parking lot, we stared up at a huge colorful *Les Misérables* banner hanging from the theater wall. "We should hang that thing on our house," I told Ramona. "That's how I feel these days. Maybe the play is about us."

But I knew it wasn't. After watching three different film versions and reading most of Victor Hugo's thick classic, I was anxious to see the stage adaptation.

I had no idea how hard it would hit me.

And how appropriate it would be for this time in our lives.

Les Misérables is the epic story of Jean Valjean, who is thrown into a French prison for stealing a loaf of bread. Released on parole after nineteen years, Valjean soon learns that his past has condemned him to the life of an outcast. The only one who befriends him is a humble bishop. Yet one night, scarred and hardened by his prison years, Valjean repays the bishop's kindness by stealing some of his valuable silver. Caught and brought back by the police, Valjean stands before the bishop, his head down, doomed to spend the rest of his days in prison.

"We found a silver plate in this man's possession," one officer says. "It is stolen from you, is it not?"

The bishop pauses for a moment. He knows Valjean's past. He wonders about his future. Then he speaks the most unexpected words: "No. I gave them to him. I'm so glad you came back because he forgot to take the silver candlesticks."

When the authorities leave, Valjean falls to his knees before the bishop. He is speechless. Tears stream down his face. Overwhelmed by this act of grace, Valjean vows that he will never be the same.

Before long, he becomes a successful factory owner, honored in his new hometown. But one day Inspector Javert, Valjean's nemesis from his prison days, comes to town. Javert, who is haunted by his own demons, has an old score to settle. And from then on, he hunts down his enemy Valjean, determined to prove him guilty and throw him back into jail. But Valjean stands by his vow. He refuses to retaliate, which confuses and infuriates Javert. In love, Valjean adopts a child and later risks his life for her fiancé. Again and again, throughout the story, he overcomes evil with good, chooses joy over bitterness, and eventually overpowers his enemy Javert with the love of God.

When the final curtain fell, I sat in the theater, moved to tears at this story of grace and redemption. Please understand that I'm not normally a weepy sort of guy. In fact, I had not cried like this since "Old Yeller" died on a Saturday afternoon when I was in fourth grade. But for the first time ever I asked myself a question that would change my life.

Who was I becoming? Valjean or Javert?

That night in our $119 hotel room, we munched chocolate-covered strawberries (compliments of the hotel), discussed the lead characters in the play, and asked ourselves: What separates those who soar from those who sink? What separates those who resign from those who rejoice?

For seven years I have sought the answer to that question.

During that time, I began asking dozens of people, many who were treading deeper water than I was, what had helped them most. Their answers were fascinating, their stories captivating. As I researched and wrote, it dawned on me that these people demonstrate five vital characteristics. Characteristics that help them walk through life as Valjean did.

I call them skunkbusters. You'll see why in a few minutes.

I believe their stories, interspersed with my own, will have you smiling until you discover five characteristics of a skunkbuster. Five characteristics that have changed my life forever.

I can't wait to tell you what they are.

SKUNKBUSTER SECRET #1

The world is full of cactus...
but we don't need to sit on one.

Ed Howe once said, "If you don't learn to laugh at trouble, you won't have anything to laugh at when you're old." Ed was right. Lately God seems to be filling my pool an inch deeper than I am tall. But I'm discovering something: When life is a tough grind, I can let the grindstone wear me down. Or polish me up. It all depends...on me. Sooner or later a storm will rage across our bow. Pushing us into uncharted waters. Stripping away the things we've clutched so tightly. Clouds come. Winds blow. But life's difficulties do not have the power to strip away one of a very few commodities we can control: our ability to choose our outlook in the worst of circumstances. It's true. Our attitude can make the worst experience painful or profitable. Our attitude can help us see that our problems usually aren't the problem. It's the way we look at them.

ONE

Who Put the Skunk in the Trunk?

"How can I believe in God when just last week I got my tongue caught in the roller of an electric typewriter?"
WOODY ALLEN

L ife's surprises rarely give ample warning. Just ask Patricia and Christopher Smith. When the couple and their two sons checked into a Maryland Comfort Inn recently, they were hoping for a warm bed, a hot bath, and maybe a few extra shampoo bottles to sneak home.

What they got was a whole lot more than they paid for.

At 1:30 A.M., Christopher awoke and got up to turn off the television. That's when he noticed that the carpet was moving. Now, if you spend any time at all in hotels, you know that this is rarely a good sign. The carpet, as it turned out, was a live ten-foot boa constrictor, which to the best of Christopher's knowledge had not been featured in the hotel's promotional literature.

At this point, he had three options:

1. Wake his wife and ask, "Honey, do you mind getting my slippers? They're in the bathroom."
2. Try to go back to sleep.
3. Check out early.

The Smiths went with option number three without bothering to check beneath the bed for forgotten items. Then they called the police. The snake was later cornered and forced into a large trash can, but not before the Smiths were cornered and forced to spend the night at a nearby 7-Eleven. Describing it as "a terrible ordeal," (they'll get no argument from me) the couple sought therapy, then filed a $1.5 million lawsuit against the motel's parent corporation, charging "negligence and intentional infliction of emotional distress."

I have to admit that, like the Smiths, I'm not real fond of reptiles. In third grade, I watched a friend put a salamander down Mrs. Hill's blouse (if you're reading this, Mrs. Hill, I trust you will remember my finer points and not seek legal counsel), but for some reason I didn't want to touch the salamander. I merely supplied the idea. But the best impractical joke I ever had the joy of participating in was launched when my friend Bobby and I discovered a small skunk waddling through a neighbor's garden one hot summer evening.

The sun was sinking just beyond the pine trees, but it was not too late for some excitement. After managing to coax the critter across the backyard with a trail of lettuce leaves, we took the keys from the ignition and opened Mr. Finney's trunk.

Now Mr. Finney was our third grade Sunday school teacher at the time, a fine accordian player, and just about the most nervous person I ever had the pleasure of sneezing behind. On Saturdays, he polished his late model Ford Fairlane until he could hardly see the initials the neighbor kids had etched into the hood. Mr. Finney was a particular man. He shined just about everything to which he was attached, and you rarely saw him with so much as a cuff link out of place.

Though we didn't know it, this was the eve of the Finney family vacation. Mr. and Mrs. Finney and their children, Joshua and Josiah, had carefully organized and packed everything they would need to have a peaceful holiday, free from the worries and cares of our small town.

As they slept, a vegetable trail led a hungry skunk past their bed of petunias, across their front yard and onto their woodbox. From there it was an easy hop into the trunk where the poor skunk hunkered down between a suitcase and a sleeping bag, nibbling on a generous portion of carrots. Bobby and I cautiously shut the lid, replaced the keys, and went to bed.

About eight o'clock the next morning, we crept back to the Finney house and waited behind a blue spruce tree while an unsuspecting Finney family filed down their front walk and climbed aboard the Fairlane, anticipation etched on their eager faces.

What happened next I will carry with me into old age.

Mr. Finney started the car and revved the engine. Then he slipped her into gear. After a tight U-turn and about thirty feet of gravel, the car screeched to a halt, spewing stones in all directions. Inside, Mr. Finney glared at his wife with a wrinkled expression. Then he turned to the children with an accusing glance. Finally he thrust open the shiny door and sniffed the air. By the time the key was in the trunk, he had his suspicions. By the time he opened it, they were confirmed. Whatever glue had held the man together until this point in his life seemed to lose its grip then. Slamming the lid down, he stood with clenched fists, kicking the bumper, his language matching the color of his car—a deep blue. We watched from behind the spruce tree, Bobby and I, wondering if we should laugh. Or cry. Or go tell our mothers.

Later that summer I was informed that the Finneys were relocating. No one quite knew why.

No one but Bobby and I.

What Mr. Finney, Mrs. Hill, and the Smiths discovered during those unforgettable moments is something that all of us humans learn as we walk through this life: Sometimes the room service is suspect. Sometimes life slithers. And sometimes it stinks.

2

Less than a year after Ramona's seizures began, I picked up the paper on my way to work, quickly dialed home, and read from the front page: "The gene that causes Huntington's disease has been discovered after a decade-long search, sparking hope a cure can be found for the deadly neurological disorder." Ramona held her breath.

Huntington's affects one in a few thousand families.

We are one of them.

At the age of thirty-nine, Ramona's oldest brother, Dennis, checked into a nursing home, his once endearing smile and warm wit are distant memories. Two of her sisters have the dread disease. And though Ramona had not been diagnosed, she was sure she was next.

As the seizures continued, we wrestled with the decision of whether or not to be tested for Huntington's. One day a wise doctor sat across from me talking of his own troubles. Of a wife whose body was riddled with cancer. He had made the diagnosis himself. "Phil," he said, his eyes growing moist, "when my worst fears were confirmed I was faced with a simple but complex decision. Run or hang in there. You must make that choice too. I've counseled many others who have walked where you walk. For most it spells divorce, followed by depression and disaster. Phil…don't go there."

I thanked him and stood to my feet.

"A tree is best measured when it's down," he told me, as I shut the door.

A few days later I sat in a coffee shop swapping jokes with a friend. As sunshine parted the clouds and flooded our table, my friend said, "You keep laughing in the midst of all this. How do you do it?"

I sipped a Coke thoughtfully. "I'm not really sure," I said. "Maybe it's the medication."

He laughed.

"I guess I'm learning that I can't control the wind, but I can adjust my sails," I said. "Some people live like they have Limburger cheese on their lips. To them the whole world stinks. I'm learning to wipe the cheese off my lips. To adjust my attitude."

Thinking about it later, I realized that the fact we're still laughing after all these years is no tribute to us. It's not a testimony to our courage. It has much to do with a simple decision made in a doctor's office. I will stay faithful to my wife and kids. And I will hang on for dear life to God. I don't always understand His ways, but I believe that He will never take me where He has not been. In the Bible He promises to give joy, peace, hope—even laughter—in the darkest night. So let's see where this adventure takes us.

Tom sees things this way. At fifty-five, he lost both of his legs in a boating accident, then watched his multimillion dollar business go down the drain. Looking up at me from his wheelchair at the back of a church one day, Tom said: "I have more questions for God than I did before this happened, but I do know that the Bible has come alive to me like never before." His eyes misted over and he looked away. His wife was standing behind him resting her hands on his wheelchair.

"Tom likes to hang verses on our fridge," she said, smiling. "We've got this big picture there of our family standing outside our headquarters in happier times. Tom wrote out some verses yesterday and stuck them below the picture." Flipping her Bible open to Habakkuk 3:17, 18, she read out loud:

> Even though the fig trees have no blossoms,
>   and there are no grapes on the vine;
>   even though the olive crop fails,

and the fields lie empty and barren;
even though the flocks die in the fields,
and the cattle barns are empty,
yet I will rejoice in the Lord!
I will be joyful in the God of my salvation.

"He also stuck a magnet below it," she laughed. "It says:

It's always darkest
just before the fridge door opens."

Tom and his wife deserve the Veteran Skunkbuster Award (VSA). What they seem to understand is something I'm just beginning to learn. The ability to laugh in the face of life's surprises comes not from knowing the future or understanding the past. But from a choice we make. One that says, "No matter what goes right, no matter what goes wrong, God is in control. And one day—maybe not tomorrow, or even next week—I'll see things His way. So I might as well just throw back my head and laugh."

Of course it can take us years to develop this attitude. Believe me, I didn't feel this way one wintry day back in ninth grade when I regretted my decision to pick up a set of barbells.

But before I tell you about it, let me issue a warning: If you're reading this late at night in a strange hotel, you may want to check the floor before we go any further.

TWO

StuffHappens

"What do people mean when they say, 'I am not afraid of God because I know He is good'? Have they never been to a dentist?"
C. S. LEWIS

I don't know about you, but I've never really liked pain.

Back in ninth grade I weighed a whopping eighty-one pounds with my pockets full of change and so I decided to beef up by doubling my celery intake and engaging in a rather rigorous exercise program which included weight lifting. My older brother Dan informed me that lifting weights above one's head kills brain cells and he didn't think I could spare many, so I opted for lying on my back and thrusting the weights into the air.

On good days I could bench press upwards of thirty pounds.

One Saturday, while doing so, those thirty pounds got away from me. I can still recall the event in vivid Technicolor—sometimes in slow motion, and often in the middle of the night.

Helplessly I watched as the barbells came crashing toward my nose. My eyes crossed. My nose cracked. And the tears came. It was the third time I had broken my nose during its short life, and to this day, when I wiggle it with one hand, it sounds like a man crunching peanuts.

"Dad," said my son not long ago, while gazing at my nose, his head cocked to one side, "at least it's not on upside-down. You'd drown in a rainstorm."

Laughter helps. But I still don't welcome pain.

That's why I'm always amazed when I hear of people who can't get enough of it. Take Jean Luc Antoni, for instance. Jean likes nothing better than snow skiing without the snow. Yes, he holds the world record for skiing down rocks. Back in 1987 he entered the record books by reaching sixty-one miles an hour zooming down a rocky slope in France. The hard part, admitted Jean Luc, was coming to a stop at the bottom without ending his career. So the ever-resourceful Frenchman erected a cardboard retaining wall so that he could crash into it when he reached rock bottom.

I think Jean lifted too many weights above his head when he was younger.

But his exploits are mild when compared with those of Reg Mellor.

At the ripe old age of seventy-two, Reg is the reigning world champion of "ferret legging," an honor most competitors would be proud to tell their grandchildren about. If they live that long. Chances are you haven't heard of ferret legging, and since you may be interested in trying it for yourself, allow me to explain the rules. Ferret legging is a contest involving (I kid you not) the tying of the competitor's trousers at the ankles and the subsequent insertion into those trousers of a pair of vicious, fur-coated, foot-long carnivores called ferrets.

Once the ferrets are firmly in your pants, the judges tighten your belt. The idea from this point onward is for you to stand still in front of the judges as long as you can while these little weasel-like critters with claws like hypodermic needles and teeth like razor blades try to chew their way out of your trousers.

Reg Mellor is the proud world record holder. He managed to keep from yelling, "Hey, who put the weasel in my pants?" for five hours, twenty-six minutes. I can just imagine Reg sitting before a roaring fire on wintry nights, telling the tale to his grandchildren:

> **GRANDPA REG:** Well, there you have it kids. And it's true as the toes on your feet. No one came close to beatin' ma record.
>
> **GRANDCHILDREN:** Wow, Grandpa, you're really something! Do you mind showing us your wooden legs again?

There is one simple principle that separates most of us from the Reg Mellors and Jean Luc Antonis of the world: We don't go looking for pain. Adventure perhaps. But not pain. In fact, we have been born with a God-given pain-resistance mechanism that flips on at a very early age, causing us to say things like, "Hey, Mama! Peel me off the stove!"

But one day we wake up to discover that Mama is no longer in the kitchen. That there's no one around to help. And to make matters worse, we didn't have to go looking for pain. It found us. Perhaps it was a knock on the door, a call on the phone, or a tap on the shoulder. And before we knew it, we were cruising down life's highway sniffing the air, wondering what was causing that awful smell, and asking why, of all the trunks in town, did it have to end up in ours?

I'm not quite sure where I got the idea that life would be one smooth slalom down a powdery ski slope. I sure didn't learn it in the nursery. Do you remember some of the poetry we used to hear there? Some of the lullabies? When I was a child of two or three, my mother rocked me gently on her lap, and hummed ever so softly the saddest of songs. Now that she has grandchildren, she loves to inflict the same punishment on their impressionable little minds. "Gramma," the children beg her, "sing the one about the cat. The one you sang Daddy back when you were on the ark."

And so she passes on the following little family heirloom:

> I lost my kitty, my pretty white kitty,
> I hunted the house all 'round.
> I looked in the cradle and under the table,
> But nowhere could kitty be found.
> So I called my dog Rover to hunt the fields over,
> To help find kitty for me.
> No dog could be kinder but he could not find her,
> Oh, where could my poor kitty be?
> So I took my hook and I went to the brook
> To see if my kitty was there.
> My kitty was found, but alas she was drowned.
> And so I gave up in despair.

It's a wonder I slept at all.

When our children were toddlers I tried to rewrite a few depressing nursery rhymes to make them suitable for sensitive children. I sang rhymes where Jack didn't break his crown. Where three blind mice got their tails fixed...and glasses too. Rhymes where Old Mother Hubbard found chips in her cupboard, where the old woman in the shoe knew exactly what to do.

The kids listened carefully and said, "Nah, Dad. Sing the one about the cat."

I suppose there are advantages to knowing from a very early age that life may not turn out as we planned. Perhaps those who listen closely in the nursery begin to understand that life will be a wild assortment of the mundane and the adventurous, the sublime and the ridiculous. That people we trust will disappoint. That friendships will fail. That although life will not turn out as we'd hoped, this is not the end of the story.

The Bible seems to echo this truth. It holds nothing back. Its stories horrify us at times, even depress us. On the rocking chair I learned of Abraham's lies, and David's unfaithfulness. Of Jezebel's dogs and Herod's treachery. And I learned of One who will never forsake us. Bible verses whispered early stay late, don't they?

Perhaps I know now why I slept so well after a ride on our rocking chair. Maybe I realized that the future would be wild, but worry was like that rocking chair. It gave us something to do. But it didn't take us anywhere.

I think I slept soundly for another reason. You see, Mom always ended the day with an old hymn. I can still hear her singing while the rain and the wind beat against our windowpanes.

> When peace like a river attendeth my way,
> When sorrows like sea billows roll.
> Whatever my lot Thou hast taught me to say,
> It is well, it is well with my soul.

I hadn't a clue what the words meant. But I do now. Such an outlook changes everything. When your nose is out of shape. When your life goes downhill. Or when you find a skunk in the trunk.

Bob and Audrey Meisner would agree. Amazingly their marriage is still intact. You'll see why in a minute. Our little adventure begins somewhere near Minneapolis, Minnesota. Appropriately it begins on a highway…

"You didn't happen to see the lid to the blender come through here, did you?"

THREE

What about Bob?

"You can't be a smart cookie if you have a crummy attitude."
JOHN MAXWELL

I first met Bob and Audrey Meisner when they invited me into their kitchen following a television program I'd been on in the city of Winnipeg, Manitoba, Canada. If you've never been to Winnipeg, well…don't go for the scenery. Go for the people. As we ate some of the finest spaghetti and meatballs this side of Italy, I listened to one of the funniest stories I'd heard in a long time. A story often punctuated by Audrey's contagious laughter (which three young children have only enhanced) and Bob's soft chuckle. Audrey is glad for that chuckle. As she puts it, "If Bob had no chuckle, I'd be in as much trouble as…well, as a person who's in a lot of trouble."

After the first few minutes of their story, I began to understand why.

Thanksgiving weekend began the way the Meisners had planned. Piling a full-size van high with mattresses, sleeping bags, and children, they drove one thousand miles through the flatlands of Manitoba to the in-laws in Michigan. It was a beautiful trip. Patchwork prairies sprinkled with lakes stretched toward the horizon. Bare poplar branches seemed to hold up their arms in surrender to winter. The children counted V-shaped columns of Canada geese deserting their homeland and heading for Florida. Neither Bob nor Audrey knew that the beauty of the first leg of their trip would stand in sharp contrast to the journey home.

The weekend was filled with relatives. And turkey. And lots of laughter. On Sunday night they said their good-byes and headed for home. Leaving at 11 P.M., they drove through the night, arriving in Minneapolis about 8:30 the next morning. Though Mom and Dad were tired, the Mall of America beckoned, and it was many hours before they watched the skylines of the Twin Cities disappear in the rearview mirror as they drove towards the setting sun.

When Audrey offered to drive, Bob clambered toward the back, where he disappeared behind some sleeping bags and drifted off to sleep.

An hour and a half later, Audrey pulled into a rest stop as quietly as she could, hoping the family would sleep on. She let the engine idle and noticed how it seemed to be missing a cylinder, which made her think of Bob's snoring coming from the back of the van.

After using the rest room, Audrey climbed back into the van, stirred some coffee, took a long sip, and pulled back onto the freeway. Two hours passed quickly as she tapped her fingers to a country gospel station and spun the dial sampling talk shows. When she arrived in Fargo, North Dakota, the kids began to wake up. But not Bob. *Wow, he's tired,* thought Audrey. *Thank God for Colombian coffee.* Her seven-year-old appeared in the rearview mirror, rubbing his eyes. "Go back to sleep, honey," said his mom.

Suddenly the peacefulness of the early morning was shattered. "Where's Daddy?"

"Very funny," said Audrey, adjusting the rearview mirror. "He's back there sleeping...isn't he?"

The children began pushing pillows aside, looking for Daddy. "Nope," said her seven-year-old, "he's not back here."

"Do you think maybe he got raptured? You know, Mom, you've been talking about when Jesus comes to get us?"

But Audrey wasn't laughing. Panic, worry, and fear overtook her as she looked for the next exit. Should she turn around and go back? She had no idea where the rest area was. Was it two hours ago? Three? "Calm down, Audrey," she told herself. "Dear Lord," she prayed, "help me find Bob. And please keep him safe, wherever he is."

Pulling into a truck stop, she picked up a pay phone and called the police. "Um...I...uh...left my husband in Minnesota," she told the officer. "At...well...at a rest stop."

There was a moment of silence. "Sorry, could you repeat that?"

After a few minutes punctuated by desperation, Audrey was able to convince him that this was no joke, that she had left her husband, but not intentionally, although he might be thinking so.

"Tell you what," said the state patrol officer, "You hang on. I'll get all the numbers of the rest stops in that area. You don't go anywhere now, ya hear?"

Audrey didn't go anywhere.

After thanking the officer for his help, she started down the list. One number after another. Each phone call was met with surprise, but no success. Almost out of hope, she dialed the very last number on the list. "Do you have a guy there who—?"

"Yaw, I shore do," said a thick Norwegian accent.

Moments later, Bob was on the phone. "Honey...I'm so sorry," said Audrey. "I didn't mean to—" Audrey started to cry. And Bob started to laugh.

Two hours earlier he had climbed out of the van to use the rest room. But when he came back, the van was gone. "Ha," said Bob out loud. "Very funny." He walked around the service area three times, expecting to find them grinning around the next corner. But they were nowhere to be found. "She wouldn't leave me like this," said Bob even louder. "Would she?"

To pass the time, Bob spent the hours washing people's windshields and praying that God would speak loudly to his wife, perhaps give her a flat tire or something. He even climbed in with a trucker, who needed some spiritual encouragement. "You know," the trucker told Bob, "this time with you was a divine appointment. I really needed this."

"Dear God," prayed Bob, "please, no more divine apppointments tonight."

Early the next morning, Bob watched the headlights of a very familiar van pull into the rest stop. He stopped cleaning windshields and breathed a huge sigh of relief. It was a return trip for Audrey. But this time she honked the horn loudly, not caring whom she woke up. "It's the first time I ever left him," she laughs now. "Believe me, it will be the last."

"We've had plenty of chuckles over this one," says Bob past a broad smile. "At first I wondered if the Rapture had taken place too. It was like something out of a horror movie. But then I thought, *Well, make the most of it.* So I did. Sometimes the only thing I can control is my outlook. My response. This was definitely one of those times."

Audrey learned a few things too. "It seems the only time I really learn is when there's nowhere else to turn but to God," she admits. "That night I learned the importance of casting all my cares on Him. They are His, and He is completely trustworthy.

"And of course I learned that it's always a good idea to count bodies before you pull out onto the freeway."

2

SKUNKBUSTERS

The man who smiles when things go wrong…
has thought of someone he can blame it on.

•

You don't get ulcers from what you eat,
But from what eats you.

•

LOST: Dog with three legs, blind in left eye,
Missing right ear, tail broken, and recently castrated.
Answers to the name of "Lucky."
SIGN ON A GROCERY STORE BULLETIN BOARD

•

Five Jell-O flavors that flopped: celery, coffee, cola, apple,
and chocolate.

•

If at first you don't succeed, so much for skydiving.

•

The best eraser in the world is a good night's sleep.

•

Years ago on *Kids Say the Darndest Things,* Art Linkletter said to a
child, "Now let me give you a situation.
You're the pilot of a commercial airliner.
And you've got 250 passengers. And you're flying to Hawaii.
You're out over the ocean and all four engines go out.
What would you do?"
The little kid stood there and thought about that one.
Then he said,
"I would press the fasten-seat-belt button and parachute."

•

"Do you ever teach your children how to get up in the morning?
Not only to get up, but how to get up?
There is a threefold technique in getting up: First, we stretch.
That gets the body going. Then, smile.
That puts the soul in the right attitude,
so that we don't start the day grumbling.
And then say, 'God loves me.' Because that sets the spirit right."
RAY STEDMAN

•

Live so the preacher won't have to lie at your funeral.

FOUR

LessonsonIce

"The juggler comes closest to our hearts when he misses the ball."
RICHARD J. NEEDHAM

Ever since I was knee-high to a referee, I've been crazy about sports. I grew up in Canada where the national religion is ice hockey; where children and adults alike attend weekly (and sometimes daily) services at their local arena and never complain about the length of the sermon. Each winter morning I could be found strapping on ice skates, tripping down the road making sparks fly all the way to the outdoor rink. There, from the time I was three years old, I learned to play hockey with the big boys. I learned to stickhandle with the best of them. To fire the puck with utmost accuracy. I also mastered the art of gliding effortlessly across a frozen sheet of ice, sometimes on my back, often crashing headfirst into the boards and waking up the following Wednesday, wearing a bewildered expression.

Maybe it's the result of getting hit with a puck one too many times, but I miss those days.

Back then Saturday night was bath night. We would file into the tub from the eldest to the youngest to scrub a week's worth of play from our bodies. This was one of those times when it didn't pay off to be the youngest of five. By the time it was my turn the water was rather murky, to say the least, and so I couldn't wait to get to the living room and gather around the Philco radio for hockey night in Canada. Ah, how I loved the roar of the crowd. The tension of overtime. Players' names which brought visions of grandeur: Gordie Howe, Frank Mahovilich, Bobby Orr, Phil Callaway. It's true, I imagined the announcer, his voice rushed with excitement: "It's Callaway, blazing down the ice…splitting the defense…he shoots…he scores! Oh, my, I have not seen anything this exciting since the Allies invaded Normandy!"

Certain that this was my calling, I pursued my dream with everything I had.

Before long I was playing with real teams in real arenas with real helmets to protect our really hard heads. Each Saturday morning we took to the ice in an empty building while the rest of the world slept. Occasionally I would look up into the bleachers to discover that today they weren't quite so empty. That Dad was there. Somehow after a long week, he had summoned the energy to haul himself out of bed just to watch me play. Dad seemed to think I displayed more talent than the Toronto Maple Leafs and the New York Rangers combined, and he would tell the world this, hollering loudly when I scored (twice that year) and clapping his big leather gloves together.

I wanted desperately to hear those gloves smack, and I couldn't wait to play professionally. I would fly Mom and Dad to the games. Buy them front row seats right behind the players. They could help the coach make important decisions.

We won only one game that year (the other team's goalie didn't show up), but Dad always encouraged me.

"Son," he would say as we walked home from the rink, Dad lugging my heavy equipment, me carrying my hockey stick, "you're not the first one to walk into a brick wall." Then he would recount historical failures: Thomas Edison struck out in his first two thousand attempts to invent the lightbulb; Henry Ford went broke five times before finally succeeding in creating a car.

"But, Dad," I said, "our Ford Meteor won't start. That's why we're walking."

"Son," he'd answer, undaunted, "never mind about that. You just be like a postage stamp. You stick to it till you get there."

In tenth grade, we stuck to it, posting our first winning season and earning the adulation of a few hundred teenage girls. It was a milestone year for me. In fact, something occurred which changed my dreams for good.

It happened like this.

Late March. The championship game. An event of such magnitude in our small town that a crowd of millions, or at least a few hundred, packed our small arena to watch the stars come out. Peering in nervous anticipation through a crack in the locker room door, I had the distinct feeling that this would be *my* night. The years of stickhandling were about to pay off. Those who had paid the scalpers twenty-five cents would not be disappointed.

But as the game progressed, my dream began to fade. In fact, as the clock ran down to the final minute, the dream had all the makings of a nightmare. We were behind 3–2 as I climbed over the boards. The final buzzer was about to sound. The fat lady was about to sing. We needed a miracle. We needed Phil Callaway.

And so I took a pass from the corner and skillfully rifled the puck past a sprawling goalie. The red goal light came on. The girls went wild. The game was tied. And I was a hero. I had scored the goal of my dreams.

Only one goal could top it. The overtime goal.

As I sat in the dressing room waiting for the ice to be cleared I eased open the locker room door for a peek at the crowd. Prepare yourselves, you lucky people. Tonight destiny is on my side. Tonight will be *my* night. You will remember me for years to come. Last week when I missed the open net, you chanted my name reassuringly:

> That's alright, that's okay.
> We still love you Callaway.

But not tonight. No need for sympathy, thank you. Only applause. Wild, exuberant, adoring applause.

And, sure enough, about five minutes into overtime I scored the winning goal. It is a moment which is forever available to me on instant replay and sometimes in slow motion. As the puck slid toward the open net, I dove, trying desperately to forge its direction. As the crowd rose to its feet, I swatted the puck across the goal line.

The red light lit.

The girls screamed.

But they were not cheering for me.

I had just scored into my own net.

I don't remember much that happened after that. In fact, the next number of years are a bit of a blur. I do remember making a beeline for the locker room where I sat down and threw a white towel over my head. And I recall the comments of my fellow teammates: "Don't worry about it, Callaway. Anyone coulda done that....if he was totally uncoordinated."

I pulled the towel around my ears to muffle the laughter. Then I unlaced my skates. And hung them up. For good.

I couldn't have known that NBA legend Michael Jordan would be cut from his high school basketball team, that Louis L 'Amour's first western was rejected 350 times by publishers, or that Albert Einstein had trouble with simple math equations (his wife helped him fill out his tax returns). It might have helped me to know that a dozen years earlier the manager of the Grand Ole Opry fired an up-and-coming singer after only one performance, advising him to go back to driving a truck. Elvis Presley pursued a singing career anyway. But I wasn't thinking of Elvis on this night.

Instead I left the building. All shook up.

Upon arriving home, I headed straight for my room. A bad case of the flu had kept Dad from the game.

"How did it go?" he asked, standing in my doorway, studying my pale face and knowing part of the answer.

"Aw, Dad," I said, hanging my head. "I can't tell you. You're sick enough."

Flopping onto my bed, I put my hands behind my head and stared at the stucco ceiling. Dad entered my room and sat beside me, saying nothing.

"Did you ever do something so stupid you wished for all the world you could go back twenty-four hours and start the day again?" I asked.

"Well," said Dad, "there was the time I shot out Old Man Henderson's headlights with my .22...and then there was—"

I interrupted him for the first time in years. Then sat up. Buried my head in my fists. And told him everything: The shock of the crowd. The shame of the dressing room. My play that would live in infamy. I didn't dare look at his face. The face of a proud dad. A dad who had some big dreams of his own for his youngest son.

There was silence for a minute. Then Dad put his hand on my knee and did the most unexpected thing in the world.

He began to laugh.

And I couldn't believe I was doing it...but I joined him.

It was the last thing either of us expected. It was the very best thing.

More than twenty years have passed since the night Dad and I sat on the edge of my bed laughing together. I remember it as the night I determined to skate again. In fact, I'm still skating. I've even managed to score a few goals over the years. Into the right net. But no goal will ever be as memorable as that overtime goal. A lifelong reminder that life's biggest victories can be found in the ruins of defeat.

For several years after that I'd wake up in a cold sweat reliving that overtime goal, but when I'd remember Dad's hand on my knee...I'd smile from ear to ear. You see, that was the night I discovered something that has made the heaviest burdens seem a whole lot lighter.

It is the simple fact that no matter what I've done, no matter where I've been, no matter how bad my world seems, my Father loves me. Isaiah said it best when he wrote:

> "For the mountains may depart and the hills disappear,
> but even then I will remain loyal to you..."
> says the LORD, who has mercy on you. (Isaiah 54:10)

Dad may not have known it, but that night he gave me a priceless glimpse into the face of my heavenly Father.

A face full of compassion, forgiveness, and grace.

A smiling face.

The face of One who laughs.

FIVE

The Choice

"There is little difference in people, but
that little difference makes a big difference.
The little difference is attitude.
The big difference is whether it is positive or negative."
CLEMENT STONE

I f you invite me to your house on a Sunday afternoon, you will soon discover one of my most annoying habits. No, I won't eat too much (unless you serve me pizza). Or chew my fingernails (unless we watch the World Series together). But, chances are, we will be sitting in your living room sipping tea and visiting when suddenly my head will start tilting to one side and my eyes will focus on the wall behind your head. It's not that I'm ignoring you or drifting off to sleep. I am simply gazing at your bookshelf.

It's a problem I developed back in early childhood. I'm sure a good psychologist could help me with it, but I already know it's my father's fault. Dad was a bookstore manager in those days, and he lined our walls with books. There were books in the hallway. Books in the kitchen. Books in my bedroom. Sometimes they ended up in the bathtub or on the roof. To this day, I believe the left side of my neck is shorter than the right simply from going to sleep each night tilted to one side, reading book titles until the darkness turned my lights out. *Treasure Island. Charles Spurgeon's Sermon Notes. Alice in Wonderland. Foxes Book of Martyrs.* Once when I was five, I stuffed six blue-covered Hardy Boy books into a heat vent. I still don't know why. The point is, no one missed them. We didn't have much cash flow, but we were never short of books at the Callaway house.

My favorites were the short story books. Perhaps it was because I was the poster boy for Attention Deficit Disorder (just ask Mrs. Dolson, my third grade teacher), but to this day I love few things more than a winter evening before a crackling fire, sipping hot chocolate and savoring a book of short stories. Whether it's mystery, science fiction, suspense, or adventure, there's something very gratifying about being entertained, surprised, and challenged all in four or five minutes.

Not long after our *Les Misérables* weekend, a friend handed me a short story that managed to accomplish all three quite nicely.

It is the story of Jerry.

Jerry is the kind of guy you love to meet in the supermarket. He always has a kind word, a funny joke, or, at the very least, a smile. It doesn't take much to bring on that smile. Jerry's happy if all of the wheels on his grocery cart are going in the same direction. If you ask him how he's doing, he's likely to reply, "If I was doing any better, I'd be twins!"

Not many restaurant managers have waiters follow them from one franchise to the next, but Jerry does. They love his attitude. A natural motivator, Jerry can tell if you're having a tough day. "Look on the bright side," he'll say. "If the sun's in your eyes, you sneeze more. It's good for you."

One day a friend said, "I don't get it, Jerry. You can't be positive all the time. How do you do it?"

Jerry replied, "Each morning I wake up and say to myself, 'Jerry, you have two choices today. You can choose to be in a good mood or you can choose to be in a bad mood.' I choose to be in a good mood. Each time something bad happens, I can choose to be a victim or I can choose to learn from it. I choose to learn from it. Every time someone comes to me complaining, I can choose to accept their complaining or I can point out the positive side of life. I choose the positive side."

"Yeah, right," the friend protested. "It's not that easy."

"Oh yes, it is," said Jerry. "Life is all about choices. When you cut away all the rest, every situation is a choice. You choose how you react to situations. You choose how people will affect your mood. You choose to be in a good mood or a bad mood. It's your choice how you live life."

One day Jerry left the back door of his restaurant open, not knowing how his theory would be put to the ultimate test.

Three thieves walked through the door that day and held Jerry at gunpoint. While trying to open the safe, his hand, shaking from nervousness, slipped from the combination lock.

The robbers panicked.

And shot him.

Jerry was rushed to the local trauma center. After eighteen hours of surgery and weeks of intensive care, he was released from the hospital with fragments of the bullets still in his body. Later, when his friend asked him how he was doing, Jerry replied, "If I were any better, I'd be twins...wanna see my scars?"

The friend declined, but asked, "Tell me, what went through your mind during the robbery?"

"The first thing that went through my mind was that I should have locked the back door," replied Jerry. "Then, as I lay on the floor, I remembered that I had two choices; I could choose to live or I could choose to die. I chose to live."

"Weren't you scared?" asked the friend.

Yes, Jerry was scared. "But the paramedics were great," he told his friend. "They kept telling me I was going to be fine. But when they wheeled me into the emergency room and I saw the expressions on the faces of the doctors and nurses, I got really scared. In their eyes, I read, 'He's a dead man.' I knew I needed to take action."

"What did you do?"

"Well, there was a big burly nurse shouting questions at me. She asked if I was allergic to anything. I said 'Yes!'"

The doctors and nurses stopped working and looked at him with concerned wrinkles on their foreheads.

Jerry took a deep breath and said loudly, "I'm allergic to bullets!"

Over their laughter Jerry told them, "Operate on me as if I am alive, not dead." And they did.

Today Jerry is still in the restaurant business. Waiters and waitresses still follow him around, basking in his encouragement, learning from his positive words of advice. Jerry will tell you without blinking that he's alive today because of the skills of some doctors, nurses, and paramedics. But by the time you finish talking with him, you'll know that he's also alive because of his amazing attitude.

🐖

Joni Eareckson Tada, who was paralyzed in a diving accident, would admire Jerry's spirit. She wrote: "With profound potential for good, suffering can also be a destroyer. Suffering can pull families together, uniting them through hardship, or it can rip them apart in selfishness and bitterness.... It all depends. On us. On how we respond."

I'm like Jerry. I'm allergic to bullets. And like Jerry, I cannot choose when or where they will hit. I would love to. But I can't. The one thing I can control is my reaction. My response. My attitude.

How about you? How are you responding to the bullets that come your way? To the skunks in your life?

Proverbs 17:22 (NIV) says, "A cheerful heart is good medicine, but a crushed spirit dries up the bones." A happy heart? Or bitter to the bone?

It all depends.

On me.

There's nothing quite like Thanksgiving Day to bring this truth to life.

"Here you go! T-bone steak, mashed potatoes and fresh asparagus! Whoops! What am I doing? This is for Mr. Cagner in room 173."

SIX

I Broke My Leg Today. At Least It Wasn't My Neck

*"At any moment in life we have the option to choose
an attitude of gratitude, a posture of grace, a commitment to joy."*
TIM HANSEL

On Thanksgiving Day my son Jeffrey came in at half-past midnight to wake me up and inform me that he couldn't sleep. Since I had to be up in six hours anyway, I groggily stumbled from my nice warm bed and my nice warm wife and took him back to his bed, stubbed my toe on it, and said in a voice three octaves above my normal one, "Jeffy, I want you to think of one hundered things you're glad about."

Looking up at me rather sleepily, he scratched his hair and asked, "Um…like what, Dad?"

I thought for a moment or two. "Well…like *me*. Are you thankful for your dad?"

"Yeah," he said. "'Cept you're sorta cranky right now."

I buried my head in his chest, hugged him tight, and listened to him laugh.

"I'm sorry, son."

Jeffrey patted my balding head. "That's okay."

"I love you."

"I love you, too."

Climbing in beside him, I whispered, "Let's start on that thankful list."

By most accounts, I shouldn't be thinking of such things. Not tonight.

A few hours ago Ramona had another seizure. I was reading a Bible storybook to the kids at the time—the story of the Good Shepherd and how He cares for His sheep. I happened to look up as she entered the room and started to reach out for me then hit the floor. As she lay unconscious I scooped her up and carried her to our bedroom, hoping to shelter the children from the horror. Later as she slept, I pulled the kids close and cried with them. Then I answered their questions as best I could.

"Is Momma gonna die?"

"I don't know, sweetie. But she loves you. And God isn't going to leave us alone."

"What's the matter with her?"

"The doctors are trying to find out. Let's pray together right now that they'll find out what's wrong. And let's thank God that she's sleeping now...that she's okay."

That night, as I pulled covers over kids, I challenged them to think of things to be glad about. But, I have to admit, I wasn't finding it so easy.

One hundred things I'm thankful for? Hmm.

It's easy to find Bible verses about giving thanks. The book of Psalms alone instructs us to "give thanks" twenty times. For instance Psalm 136:1 says:

> Give thanks to the LORD, for he is good!
> His faithful love endures forever.

But how does one write out a "Stuff I'm Thankful For" list when you've just watched your wife come back from the brink of death for the hundredth time, and you're worried about tomorrow, and you're wondering about your kids?

If we're really honest, we don't always feel like giving thanks, do we? You sit down to fill out a "Stuff I'm Thankful For" list, but all that comes out is: I'm thankful for my job. No, wait a minute, scratch that. My coworkers are like blisters. They only show up when all the work is done. Besides, my boss treats me like an imbecile and I'd do anything to be able to go fishing tomorrow. Or…I'm thankful for my spouse. Except, the meal she cooked today should have gone straight into the compost. Let's see now…the kids? Well, on Thursday my daughter parked the car in the garage…without putting up the garage door. On second thought, perhaps I'll work on my "To Do" list.

And then one day we come upon 1 Thessalonians 5:16–18, the words of the apostle Paul, a guy who suffered enough beatings and shipwrecks and imprisonments to make the cover of *The Guinness Book of World Records*:

> Always be joyful. Keep on praying. No matter what happens, always be thankful, for this is God's will for you who belong to Christ Jesus.

I think Paul would agree that the most genuine gratitude is shown by those who don't always feel like showing it. That those who give thanks for the speed bumps in life are better able to see them from God's perspective. So tonight, as my youngest child loses a battle with his eyelids, I tell God—and him—a few of the things I have to be thankful for…

I'm thankful for Thanksgiving Day.

I'm glad we don't eat turkey every day of the year. We'd all look like the Goodyear blimp by Christmas.

I'm glad for memories of an afternoon of touch football at the

Callaway Annual Thanksgiving Day Oldtimer's Game (CATDOG) and coming to the table sweating and eager and prepared to dodge my brother's spoonful of mashed potatoes which last year struck me SPLAT! on the forehead. Although none of us can run as fast anymore, we still enjoy that classic football game. And although the food fights are a thing of the past, I'm still childlike enough to hold a spoonful of my wife's sage dressing and measure the distance to Grandpa's glistening head and wonder just for a moment what it would be like to release the dressing.

I'm thankful for my ability to make bread now that we have a bread-making machine. Ramona's health troubles have forced me into the kitchen to exercise my food preparatory muscles a little more often. Several times while she has been sleeping, the kids and I have enjoyed cake and ice cream for breakfast—delicacies, I keep reminding myself, which contain the four basic food groups: milk, eggs, flour, and artificial flavoring.

I'm glad that although things aren't what I'd like them to be, they're not as bad as they could be. I'm thankful for a wife who loves me and in the toughest of times has been faithful, loving, and gentle.

I'm thankful that my hope is not fixed on the stuff of this earth. That I've got more than tomorrow to look forward to. I've got eternity.

I'm thankful for a storm which blew in after our Classic, reminding me that in the cold we seem to huddle together, needing each other more.

I'm thankful I've never gone hungry. Except when dieting.

I'm thankful for the dark. It's the only time I can see the stars.

I'm thankful for Someone to thank.

And for three wonderful children. God's gifts to me. They surround us with laughter, energy, mischief, and love.

I'm thankful that all of them have finally gone to sleep.

I think I will too.

SKUNKBUSTERS

Just before saying the Thanksgiving dinner blessing, my older brother asked Jeffrey—who was busy stuffing his face with turkey—if he had prayed yet. Jeffrey said past a mouthful of his favorite food, "Yep. I prayed to myself."

Here are a few other Thanksgiving prayers children have offered…to God:

Dear God, Thanks for letting my goldfish live a long life.
JUSTIN, AGE 6

•

Dear God, Thank you for inventing my parents.
ADAM, AGE 5

•

God, Thank you for having my sister, and
for letting me have my hamster.
LOUIS, AGE 6

•

Thank you, God, for making a nice sun and a nice rainbow
and a nice Mom.
YONI, AGE 6

•

Dear God, Thank you for the air.
SHAWN, AGE 7

•

Dear God, I am so glad you are always looking out for me.

MAX, AGE 6

•

Whatever is good and perfect comes to us from God above, who created all heaven's lights.

JAMES 1:17

•

Thankfulness is the soil in which joy grows strong.

SEVEN

The Envelope, Please

*"God's wisest saints are often people who endure pain
rather than escape it."*
CHARLES R. SWINDOLL

Hollywood does it. Nashville too. In long and drawn-out ceremonies, film and record industries stumble all over themselves to pat backs and present statues to superstars. But too often our culture honors its celebrities and forgets its saints. We decorate the stars and shelve the servants. Thankfully, it's not always the case. The other day I had the honor of presenting a rather unusual award on the campus of Prairie Bible Institute.

It was an austere weekend. Dignitaries had gathered from around the world to witness the conferring of degrees upon worthy students. In the midst of it all, I was asked to present a humor award to a retiring faculty member known for his laughter amid tough times. I stood to my feet, wondering how the audience would respond.

"It gives me no small degree of goose bumps to present an award to a man who is no stranger among us," I began, "although we sometimes wish he were…after some of the jokes he tells. Dr. Gerald Wheatley stopped me the other day and said, 'Did you hear the one about the two cannibals who were eating a clown? One says to the other, "Does this taste funny to you?"' Dr. Wheatley can tell cannibal jokes at the dinner table until your six-ounce steak does not look so appealing. Jokes like, 'What did the cannibal get when he was late for breakfast? The cold shoulder.' Or 'What is a cannibal's favorite game? Swallow the leader.' His favorite is about the cannibal who loved fast food. He ordered a pizza with everybody on it."

Although the jokes were a little corny, everyone seemed to be smiling.

"Dr. Wheatley," I continued, "we are thankful for a man who takes God seriously, but who also believes that life is too serious not to spend a good deal of it laughing. To you I present two awards.

"First," I said, handing this distinguished professor a box of wheat crackers, "the Cracked Wheatley Award, for outstanding service, especially during coffee time in the faculty lounge. G. K. Chesterton once said that angels can fly because they take themselves lightly. So, it seems, can you. Thanks for the jokes. Thanks for your example. Thanks for the reminder that those who laugh, last. And that Christians do not need to look like they were baptized in lemon juice."

Then I took out a healthy bunch of bananas.

"You once told me that politicians and bananas are alike. They are yellow, crooked, and they all hang together. So I would like to present you with the Ripe Banana Award." Laughter filled the building. "Dr. Wheatley," I said in conclusion, "may you live long enough to be older than your jokes."

Not everyone who has suffered on this earth will have a plaque or a bunch of ripe bananas to show for it. But if I could, I'd like to confer five more Skunkbuster Awards on the following people. Chances are you haven't met them yet. So let me introduce you to some ordinary folk who came up smiling when their canoes capsized. The envelope please…

❧

Four years ago life was just shy of perfect for Carol McMillan. At age seventy-five, the Miami, Florida, resident enjoyed good health, a fifty-four year marriage, a son who had just turned thirty, and three grandchildren, whom she believed to be the smartest, most beautiful kids in the world. But within three months her world turned upside-down. It started on a November day when her husband, a cancer victim, said good-bye for the very last time. One month later, just after Christmas, the news worsened. Her only son had taken his own life, leaving behind three beautiful children. Children with far too many questions. While she was grieving, her house was broken into and most of her valuables taken. "A dark cloud enveloped my life," Carol told me.

Feeling alone, abandoned, and afraid, she sat at her piano by the hour playing through an old hymnbook, the tears streaming down her face. One day while doing the dishes, a voice on the radio seemed to part the clouds and reach through: "Yesterday is history," said the voice, "Tomorrow is a mystery. But today is a gift. That's why we call it the Present."

For the first time in months, a smile stole across Carol's face. "The phrase marked a turning point for me," she said later. "Yesterday is gone. Tomorrow may never arrive. But I have the gift of today. I guess you could say I had a faith lift that day. And a face lift too!" For the first time in over a year, Carol began going to church again. And a few Sundays ago, a young dashingly handsome seventy-three-year-old asked her out. Carol said, "Yes."

One Sunday night the two sat in her living room as she played through that old hymnal. "You play beautifully," he told her. "I'm glad the piano was too big for those thieves to carry away."

When she visited her ninety-six-year-old mother in a nursing home and told her that she was dating, Carol couldn't help but laugh at her response. "I think you're robbing the cradle!" said her mother, with a twinkle in her eye.

I was flying home from a five-day business trip, looking forward to taking my kids to dinner at their favorite hamburger joint, Spunkys. Soon, however, I heard the pilot say, "Sorry, folks, we're going to have a slight delay this morning. We've got oil leaking out of engine number two. It shouldn't take more than an hour to tidy things up." A little later, he was back. "Just keep relaxing, folks," he said. "The mechanics are working on engine number two." When he made a third announcement, I was getting worried about making my connecting flight.

As time rolled by, I started counting the pilot's announcements. The fourth: "We have to let several other planes go ahead of us." The fifth: "We're waiting for a runway to clear." Eleven announcements and many hours later we arrived in Chicago, where, despite the pilot's reassurances, I discovered that I wouldn't arrive home until after the kids were in bed.

When I finally came through the door that night, tired and exhausted, all three kids were in their pajamas, excited to see me. "Dad, we're hungry," they said.

"How about a Spunky burger, kids?"

"Yeah!"

So we jumped in the car, pajamas and all. It wasn't my original plan—but it worked. In fact, the kids had far more fun than if we'd gone three or four hours earlier. By turning a disappointment on its head, we made a memory that will last a lifetime.

I love what Kent Hughes says: "God is not so much interested in whether we reach our destination as in how we try to get there. To us arrival is everything, but to God the journey is most important, for it is in the journey that we are perfected, and it is in hardships that He is glorified as we trust Him."

DAVID SANFORD, PORTLAND, OREGON

It's been quite a year. Four months ago there were seven people and two dogs living in our house. Today only my husband and I live here. Our three children, a Swedish exchange student, and my father-in-law have all moved out. To complicate matters, my mother was recently diagnosed with Alzheimer's.

Years ago I decided that I can't control my circumstances but I can choose my attitude. So I decided to look for something positive in each day. Some days it's a sunset, the unexpected meeting of an out-of-town friend, a colored picture from a ten-year-old, the dogs' joy in greeting me when I come home, or simply reading "Calvin & Hobbes" before bedtime. Laughter makes for a good sleep. I'm also learning that it makes for a fuller house.

JENNIFER BROWN, SWAN RIVER, MANITOBA

To me, diabetes means taking two insulin shots a day, watching what I eat and when I eat it, and checking my blood four times a day to make sure my sugar levels don't resemble the sap in a maple tree. Since the age of seven, this has been my daily routine. Twenty-five thousand injections later, the complications of this disease are evident. My kidneys have failed and I have been on hemodialysis for the last two years. The transplant has been slow in coming.

Going three times a week to the hospital, four hours each visit, watching one hundred liters of blood go in and out of your body through tubes, filters, and machines is no picnic—unless you're Dracula. But in the midst of it all I have found strength in some solid friendships and a strong marriage. One thing, however, has been particularly difficult. Since my body is never toxin-free and the drugs I'm on affect my ability to be alert in the pew, it's even tougher to sit still in church than when I was a boy. I discussed this problem with our pastor one evening. He suggested that I should feel free to leave at any time or to stretch out on the pew if there's room.

One Sunday morning, the drugs really kicked in and I had no choice but to stretch out. That's when the congregation found out about my snoring problem! Fortunately it's not the lawn mower variety, but a visitor later said, "I've seen people fall asleep during a sermon before. But I've never seen anyone do so lying down!"

HOWARD BLANK, CALGARY, ALBERTA

This week my wife and I celebrated our sixty-first anniversary in the nursing home where we live. Not long ago we got permission to put a bulletin board outside our room. This week I put these words there, large enough for some of the older ones to see: "Cherish Today."

RALPH JOHNSON, PITTSBURGH, PENNSYLVANIA

Every once in a while, just for kicks, Dr. Fernlock liked to amplify his drill through the office's stereo system.

SKUNKBUSTER SECRET #2

When opportunity knocks,
don't complain about the noise.

Recently I met Mary Jean, an outgoing forty-five-year-old who's faced her share of obstacles. "I'm so short," she laughed as she reached up to shake my hand, "that they gave me a periscope with my driver's license." As we talked I noticed that Mary Jean was watching my lips move. I asked if I had mustard on them. "No," she smiled, "I'm deaf. My best friend is deaf, too. We were out for a walk once and I said, 'It sure is windy today,' and my friend answered, 'No, it's Thursday.' I said, 'Me too, let's go get a drink.'"

Six months ago Mary Jean wasn't laughing. Six months ago, her husband of twenty-eight years walked out the door. "He's in Florida now," she said, looking down, "pursuing other interests." Then the smile returned. "A month ago I put a note in each mailbox on our street. It said, 'I'm the lady in the blue house. Don't worry, I'm not crazy. I just want you to know that I'm praying for you.' I've never had so many calls, so many visitors. A widow down the street came by to ask what gets me through. Yesterday a pregnant teen knocked on my door. 'I thought you'd understand,' she said."

In some, pain produces resentment, anger, and negativity. They smell flowers…and look around for a funeral. But in Mary Jean pain has produced an opportunity. New chances for compassion to spill over into action. She's less likely to run from the suffering of others now. More likely to stoop than stare. More likely to listen than offer grand advice. She knows roses have thorns. She's felt them. But she also knows firsthand that a rose can bring a smile. So she picks them carefully. And passes them along.

EIGHT

Help! We're Breaking Out in Toddlers!

"Either that wallpaper goes, or I do."
REPORTEDLY THE LAST WORDS OF HUMORIST OSCAR WILDE

The wife of an army colonel had endured an all-night flight across the Atlantic to meet her husband at his latest military assignment. She arrived at Rhein-Main Air Base in Germany with nine good reasons to be exhausted. As she exited the plane all nine of them followed her—not a one over the age of eleven.

Collecting their many suitcases, the entourage filed noisily into the cramped customs area. A young official stared at them in wide-eyed disbelief.

"Ma'am," he said, "do all these children belong to you?"

"Yes, sir," she said with a sigh. "They're all mine."

"Well, how about this luggage. Is it all yours?"

"Yes, sir," she said with a nod. "It's mine too."

"Ma'am," he continued, "do you have in your possession any weapons, contraband, or illegal drugs?"

"Sir," she calmly replied, "if I had any of those items I would have used them by now."

Perhaps you can identify with this weary saint. My wife and I certainly can. After having three children in three years, we decided to pick up some child-rearing books. One of them advised us that we should learn early to set limits on our children. It made perfect sense to us. So we decided our limit was three.

Looking back, I thank God that we didn't stop at two. After the following story, I think you'll understand why.

On a September day nine years ago I sat at the dinner table with my wife and two very small children. It had been a good day and I bowed my head and prayed out loud: "Lord, I thank you for your abundant goodness to us. For the ham and potatoes and these two children. For a good night's rest and enough money to pay the hospital bills. We are blessed, Lord. Continue to bless us abundantly, we pray. In Jesus' name, amen."

I was met with silence when I looked up. Ramona stared at me with a very strained expression on her face, as if she were deciding whether to laugh or cry. I dove fork-first into the potatoes. "So, how did your day go?" I asked.

There was more silence. I looked up to see tears forming in Ramona's eyes.

"What is it?" I was midway through a potato.

"Nothing. You go ahead and eat. I'm not so thankful."

"Come on," I said through a full mouth. "Whuch's wong?"

"Honey…" she looked down momentarily. "I…I…I'm…pregnant."

I was seized by a choking reflex. Coughing loudly, I reached for a glass of milk and downed it like a whiskey-drinker in an old western. Then I calmly responded: "WHAT? THAT'S IMPOSSIBLE! RACHAEL IS THREE DAYS OLD!"

"Three MONTHS old," she corrected me.

"But it can't be. You're joking, aren't you? Ha, that's a good one, honey. Please pass the ham."

There was more silence. Tears had begun to reach her down-turned smile.

"I was just starting to feel like I could get up in the morning," she said quietly, staring out the window at the setting sun.

I looked at my plate and stabbed the potato. Hard. I hadn't been this surprised since the time I watched a mystery movie where the kind old lady who lived behind the picket fence and waved to the school bus each morning poisoned her husband's tea.

The following June we found ourselves in the maternity ward. Thirty-three weeks had passed since that dinner table surprise. Gathered with us to witness this most private of events was the doctor, his assistant, the obstetrician, the pediatrician, the anesthesiologist, the janitor, the janitor's understudy, and three premed students. I felt like asking why we didn't just put the event on CNN. But Ramona didn't seem to notice. You see, Jeffrey Paul had just been born. He came into the world much like our other two, but you didn't need an eighth-grade diploma to see that he would be very different. From week one Jeffrey let us know long into the night that he was not pleased to be here. This was not his decision and someone else should pay.

His whimper could melt your heart, but his piercing howl could peel wallpaper. "He's colicky," explained my wife. "I was when I was his age, and apparently you were, too." I asked her if having this information had ever helped anyone.

By the time Jeffrey learned to use a pacifier, another problem had arisen: The child was—well—aggressive, an ideal candidate for presidency of the Society for the Strong-Willed. If he wanted something, he would flag down a freight train to get it.

"You said once that children are gifts from heaven," said Ramona one evening as she reclined on the couch, gasping for air. "I understand now why God gave this one away." Thankfully she was joking, but those were busy days. It was like running a twenty-four-hour day care center. Our diaper bill exceeded the gross annual income of some small countries. Cleaning house was like shoveling snow in a blizzard. One winter day I said to Ramona, "Show me a child who has just been dressed in multiple layers of warm clothing, mittened, and squeezed into a pair of ice skates…and I'll show you a child who has to go to the bathroom."

One Sunday after church we stood in a restaurant cafeteria line and watched in horror as Jeffrey reached out and punched a total stranger—perhaps for the sheer joy of watching her bend over to rub her knee.

"Do you suppose we got the wrong one?" I ventured that afternoon. "You know, sometimes the baskets get swapped."

"Naw," my wife responded. "He's too much like you."

She was right.

My parents were old enough to pay the maternity bills with old-age pension checks when I was born. Ladies in our small town talked about it in front of my mother's back: "What are you doing having another one when your biological clock is blinking midnight?" one asked.

Some referred to me as the caboose.

An afterthought.

My high school teachers called me a mistake.

But I never heard those words from Mom and Dad. Instead, I heard words like, "I love you" and "I don't know what I'd do without you." And, just as importantly, I was shown that love. I was loved. Just like the rest.

It will be the same with Jeffrey. Not because it's all we know, or because it's the noble thing. But because of a simple truth I hope I never forget: God's grace always accompanies life's surprises.

And because it's true: I can't imagine life without this little guy. Life without his laugh. Life without his smile. I wish you could meet him. Jeffrey has the appetite of a horse, the curiosity of a cat, the energy of an atom bomb, and the lungs of an opera singer. I've locked him out of my study a few times, but I'll never lock him out of my heart. When I arrive home from work he attacks me with a viselike hug. He loves to wrestle me to the carpet. And tickle me when I'm down. Sometimes when my dreams lay broken at my feet and my world is a mess, Jeffrey comes along and puts it back together with three magic words: "Love ya, Dad." In the midst of a busy, hectic schedule, God sent a little child to teach me how to laugh again.

One day a few years ago, as we drove home from church, he stood in the backseat singing loudly, "Love blinded me...as far as I can see...love blinded me." I smiled at Ramona and asked Jeffrey where he learned that song. "That's what you grown-ups were singin' in church," he said. As we sat at the dinner table one night, he told us, "The thing I like best about Sunday school is the sinning."

It's tough to listen to our children without laughing. It's tough to listen without learning.

And if we listen hard enough, we just may learn a very important lesson when it comes to surprises: When God sends one our way, embrace it. When opportunity knocks, don't complain about the noise. Instead, pass God's grace along.

NINE

The Last Shoe Box

"If you ever think you're too small to be effective,
you've never been in bed with a mosquito."
ANITA RODDICK

I was only four when Mrs. Muddle adopted me for a week. With my mother in the hospital and my father needing help, she must have seen me pulling my wagon complete with a cargo of grasshoppers along Eighth Avenue in the tiny town of Three Hills, looking sad and forlorn. And so she took me in. That's what neighbors did in those days. Although I may have been a handful, Mrs. Muddle smiled a lot during that week. A four-year-old doesn't remember much. But he remembers a smile. I wasn't her first child. She had five others. But none of them seemed to mind my intrusion.

My own Dad came along and tucked me in each night, so I knew all would be well. But one day it wasn't. One day they tell me that I found a fresh jar of sweet pickles in Mrs. Muddle's fridge. By the time I was full, the jar was empty. Mrs. Muddle didn't say much, just held my little forehead as I transferred those sweet pickles from my stomach to her sink. She had every right to say, "Ha! It serves you right, you gluttonous little orphan." But she didn't. I was worth more than a jar of pickles to her, I suppose. And so I enjoyed that week. I enjoyed her smile. But I can't face sweet pickles to this day.

Thirty-three years passed.

On a Friday afternoon a month before Christmas I joined three hundred others in an overflowing church to celebrate Mrs. Muddle's life. And mourn her passing. At the front beneath a rugged wooden cross sat a few hundred brightly wrapped shoe boxes, waiting for December and the volunteers at Samaritan's Purse to scatter them Santalike around the world. The coordinator for Operation Christmas Child in our community is Tony Hanson. Mr. Hanson is one of those elderly people who views retirement as an opportunity to do things he always wanted to do before. When he grows up, he wants to be a child, he'll tell you. And so he laughs often, and his wrinkles are in all the right places. He's even apt to tell you a joke or two or toss a wise saying your way when you shake hands after church: "He who laughs last, thinks slowest," is one of them.

Standing to his feet during the funeral, Mr. Hanson took one of the boxes to the pulpit and smiled at the crowd. "This is Mrs. Muddle's shoe box," he said, lifting the lid and pulling out a freshly pressed shirt. "Don't worry, I haven't opened any of the other boxes."

The box was marked for a boy ten to fourteen years old. In it were clothes, a Bible, and things boys the world over seem to enjoy. It also contained a handwritten note. "Do you mind if I open it?" asked Mr. Hanson. The family nodded its eager approval.

I sat near the back, listening as he read the last words Mrs. Muddle wrote. Words that left me and a few hundred others fighting back the tears.

Dear friend,

I hope you enjoy this gift box. It comes with my love to you. I am sick and very weak now, so do not write well. I have three granddaughters and seven grandsons and I love them all. My prayer is that they will all come to know Jesus as their Savior. I believe they have accepted Him, but not all are living for Him. I pray you will accept Him too. I am your new Grandma—I'm eighty-five years old.

With my love,

Honor Muddle.

All kinds of people have impacted me through the years. Some are preachers. Some are writers. Others are relatives. And one was a faithful wife and mother with a simple philosophy: When you see a need, meet it.

Ten years ago, when I was staring down the barrel of a job I felt vastly underqualified for—as editor of *Servant* magazine—one of the first things I did was ask about twenty retired people to pray for me. Mrs. Muddle was one who said yes. When I met her from time to time in the grocery store or on the street she would remind me that she was praying for me. And a few times she said, "I pray for you every day."

A few weeks after her beloved husband passed away, she reminded me, "I pray for you every day."

When her health was failing and she knew her time was short, Mrs. Muddle was praying for me.

One night she called our pastor. Pastor John had been sick for a few days. In fact, a flu bug had laid him out so flat that he could barely enjoy Monday night football. "How are you doing?" Mrs. Muddle asked him.

"I'm okay," he responded, recounting a few of his aches and pains, but trying not to give her an organ recital.

"I just wanted to see how you were feeling so I would know how to pray," she said. They talked for fifteen minutes before John found out that she was calling him from a hospital bed.

I can't read Philippians 2:3–4 without thinking of Mrs. Muddle's example:

Don't be selfish; don't live to make a good impression on others. Be humble, thinking of others as better than yourself. Don't think only about your own interests, but be interested in others, too, and what they are doing.

Reminds me of another story. It happened a few years ago at the Special Olympics in Seattle. Nine contestants, all physically or mentally disabled, assembled at the starting line for the 100-yard dash. The contestants waited. The crowd watched. The gun sounded. It wasn't exactly a dash, but all nine ran the best they could. Hoping to finish. Hoping to win. Suddenly one of them stumbled on the asphalt, tumbled over, and began to cry.

The other eight heard his cry. They slowed down and looked back. Then every one of them stopped, turned around, and went back to get him.

A girl with Down's syndrome bent over and kissed him. "This will make it better," she said sweetly. A few helped him up. Then all nine linked arms and walked across the finish line.

Together.

Everyone in the stadium stood. The ovation went on for several minutes. People who were there still tell this story. Why? Because joy is one of the few things that is multiplied when it's divided. Because those who bring sunshine to the lives of others can't keep it from shining on themselves.

I asked Mrs. Muddle once what helped her during tough times. "Oh," she said simply, "life is too short to live it for yourself."

That's the way she lived.

That's the way she died.

Helping people like me run the race.

I'll never look at a jar of sweet pickles without thinking of that one word: Others.

SKUNKBUSTERS

"There's no problem so big that I can't run away from it."
CHARLIE BROWN

•

"Next week there can't be any crisis. My schedule is already full."
HENRY A. KISSINGER

•

Those who say nothing is impossible
have yet to walk through a revolving door with toddlers.

•

"My ancestors told me to have many children."
THUMA NZUMAKASE, FATHER OF 139

•

If at first you don't succeed,
You're just like the rest of us.

•

I take a ninety-year-old lady to church every Sunday. Last week she told me a story that's kept her laughing lately. When her great-grandchild's dog died she tried to comfort him as best she could. "Buffy was a good dog and I'm sure he's in heaven with God." Her grandchild stopped crying, looked up at her and said with disgust, "What's God gonna do with a dead dog?"

CHRISTINA SCHAWILKE, ABBOTSFORD, BRITISH COLUMBIA

•

If you're busy rowing the boat,
you won't have time to rock it.

•

So live that you won't be ashamed to
sell your parrot to the town gossip.

•

The difference between outlaws and in-laws:
Outlaws don't promise to pay it back.

•

Sound travels slowly.
Things you tell your kids don't reach them until they're forty.

•

"My wife made me a millionaire. I used to have three million."
HOCKEY HALL OF FAMER BOBBY HULL

•

"Jesus did not come to explain away suffering or remove it.
He came to fill it with His presence."
PAUL CLAUDEL

•

"If you cling to your life, you will lose it;
but if you give it up for me, you will find it."
JESUS IN MATTHEW 10:39

TEN

Reluctant Hero

*"Never give in! Never give in! Never! Never! Never! Never!
In anything great or small, large or petty—never give in
except to convictions of honor and good sense."*
SIR WINSTON CHURCHILL, WHO SMOKED OVER 300,000 CIGARS

erhaps it is no coincidence that the words "report card" and "repentance" start with the same letters. Just yesterday our children brought home their envelopes and haltingly handed us their report cards. There was no drum roll. No Grammy Award-like fanfare. No thank-you speeches. Today we visited their teachers. And asked for forgiveness.

I keep telling my wife that there are more important things than A's in mathematics. That we're more concerned with developing the "I's, D's, and C's": integrity, diligence, and character. "Character?" she responds, "We're partway there, honey. We're developing characters."

As you may know, part of the risk of parenthood is that you're never quite sure what your kids are going to write, think, say, or smash. One day Rachael lined her dolls up on the bed and placed a piece of paper and a pencil before each one. "Whatcha doing?" I asked her, poking my nose through her open door. "Playing school," she answered. "I'm the teacher…and these are my *prisoners*."

Some time ago, Ramona was visiting a former friend of ours who by her own admission had been struggling with her waistline. In fact, she'd been struggling from diet to diet and from fridge to fridge. Jeffrey, who was four at the time, looked across the table at this dear lady, and said with sincerity, "You know, dinosaurs are even bigger than you."

And you wondered why I referred to her as a former friend.

Of course, there are moments when kids surprise us in another way. Moments that make us proud to be their parents. In sixth grade, Stephen's teacher asked the students to write down the name of their hero. One child wrote "Bart Simpson." Another wrote "Mother Teresa." Stephen wrote two simple words on a page: "My dad."

I raised his allowance that day.

Decided to take him to Disney World.

Bought the child mutual funds.

Of course I'm kidding. But his flattering words reminded me that God is in the business of building character into characters. And He can do that with the most unlikely candidates.

Let me tell you about one of those characters.

One of my heroes. A guy named Doug.

If they gave out "Most Likely to Fail" awards in high school, Doug Nichols would have been handed his even before the vote.

Born in 1942—the same year his father left home for another woman—Doug was raised by his mother and grandfather. Before long he was known as a troublemaker, something that earned him a high school diploma six months earlier than his classmates.

"Hey Doug," said the principal one day, "have I got a deal for you!"

The tall skinny teen stood before his superior uneasily, wondering if the deal included a firing squad.

"You promise not to come back after Christmas, and I'll give you your diploma now."

Doug smiled. Laughed. And eagerly accepted.

By the time he entered college, Doug was majoring in two subjects: women and alcohol. His late night exploits were well known, his reputation widespread. You want fun, talk to Nichols. Whatever he does, he holds nothing back.

One night during finals week, he returned to his room from a night on the town. With the help of both walls he stumbled down a long and shifting hallway.

There stood a classmate, Hank Jaegers.

"Hey Doug," said Hank, "how about some coffee?"

Inside Jaegers' room, between long sips of very thick liquid, Nichols listened as his new friend told him an old, old story. The story of Someone who would rather die than live without him. The coffee sobered Doug. The story changed his life. He sat in a folding chair, shaking his head. *Jesus loves me?* At 4:30 in the morning in a small dorm room in California, Doug got on his knees and asked God to change him for good. "I was full of coffee," he recalls, "but I understood that Jesus died so I could live with Him, so I trusted Christ."

For the first time in his life, Doug had a Father. The adventure had just begun.

The next morning, the new convert to Christianity armed himself with a huge black Thompson Chain Reference Bible, but soon discovered a problem. His marks had been slipping ever since kindergarten and he couldn't read a paragraph.

One year later a letter arrived from Hank Jaegers. He was

studying at Prairie Bible College in Canada. "Why don't you join me?" asked Hank.

But Jaegers had no idea what it would cost his friend. "By that time I was engaged to be married," says Nichols, "and my fiancée's father told me to make a choice. I could stay in California and have a brand-new Cadillac, a fancy house, and a prosperous business. Or I could go to Bible college up with the polar bears." When Doug decided on the latter, his fiancée turned her back and dumped him.

"That Cadillac's in a junkyard somewhere," he laughs. "And I don't know about the girl."

His poor reading and writing skills nearly did him in at Bible college. But in 1966 he somehow made it to graduation, set his determined face toward the mission field, and ran smack into a major barrier. His soiled past and poor marks in school caused thirty mission agencies to turn him down. Finally Operation Mobilization said yes. "OM accepts anyone," jokes Nichols.

While learning the Tagalog language, the frustration continued. "Doug," said a teacher after hours of frustration, "do you know what 'Walang utak' means?"

"No."

"I didn't think so. It means 'no brains!'"

But Doug was smart enough not to quit. During twenty years in the Philippines, together with his Bible college sweetheart, he learned a new language, started churches, and founded a new mission, Action International. Today its 130 missionaries feed, clothe, and love thousands of street children around the world.

While preaching in India many years ago, Doug began to cough. A doctor diagnosed him with acute tuberculosis and sent him to a sanitarium to recuperate. Nichols offered his fellow patients gospel booklets. All of them refused. Dejected, the young preacher began to despair. One night as he lay awake, unable to sleep because of a raspy cough, he noticed an old man trying to leave his bed, only to fall back, exhausted and crying. The stench from the old man's bed the next morning brought loud insults from fellow patients. He had been unsuccessful in trying to get up and go to the rest room. Nurses roughly changed his bedding. One slapped him. Nichols watched as the old man curled up in a ball and wept.

The next morning about 2:00 A.M., Doug awoke again. The old man was trying to get out of bed. This time, without thinking, Doug left his bed, lifted the frail patient and carried him to the bathroom. When he had finished, Doug carried him back to bed.

Jabbering in a language Doug did not understand, the old man smiled profusely, then kissed him gently on the cheek.

In the morning, Doug awakened to a steaming cup of tea served to him by another patient who spoke no English. After serving the tea, the patient motioned to Doug that he would like a booklet.

"Throughout the day," says Doug, "people came to me, asking for gospel booklets." There were nurses. Doctors. Hospital interns. Over the next few days, several came by to tell Doug that they had made the same decision he had one coffee-soaked night in California.

"I simply took an old man to the bathroom," smiles Doug. "Anyone can do that."

Six years ago, Doug listened again to a doctor's prognosis. "You have colon cancer, Doug. After radiation and chemotherapy you have a 30 percent chance of recovery."

"You mean I have a 70 percent chance of dying?" Nichols corrected him.

"Uh...I wouldn't put it that way."

Today Doug is more alive than ever. But he's hard to find. We stay in touch by e-mail. If he's not praying over squatters on a garbage dump in Manila, he might be hugging a dying child in a refugee camp. If he's not visiting one of his two adopted Filipino children, he may be celebrating the fact that doctors are shaking their heads. The cancer seems to have vanished.

Many years ago as the body of David Livingstone, celebrated missionary doctor to Africa, was carried through the streets of London on its way to a final resting place in Westminster Abbey, thousands of people the world over mourned his passing.

One man in particular wept openly.

A friend gently consoled him, asking if he had known Livingstone personally. "I weep not for Livingstone, but for myself," the man said. "He lived and died for something. I have lived for nothing."

Livingstone's life motto was this: "I will place no value on anything I have or possess, except in its relationship to the kingdom of God."

David Livingstone lived that way. So does Doug Nichols.

Doug knows the future is cloudy. The cancer could return at any time. But this fireball that God transformed from an out-of-control college kid to a mission leader still believes what he told the doctor the day cancer stared him in the face for the first time. "Let me tell you something, Doc," said Nichols, a broad smile crossing his face. "I may have a 70 percent chance of dying. But whatever happens, I have a 100 percent chance of going to heaven."

And when he gets there a report card will be waiting. It may be the first one he's ever received with these two words: "Well done."

ELEVEN

The Long Good-Bye

"God will not look you over for medals, degrees, or diplomas, but for scars."
ELBERT GREEN HUBBARD (1856–1915)

I f, some Sunday morning, you find yourself smack dab in the middle of a Canadian winter, shivering your way to a small church on the edge of our town, you will have the privilege of basking in one of the warmest smiles this side of Hawaii. Avonelle Martin is known for that smile, its accompanying laugh, and her generous words of encouragement. She seems to have a sixth sense when it comes to picking out people who need a kind word, some prayer, or a fresh box of chocolates.

This past Christmas our doorbell rang.

In came Avonelle with a package.

"The children didn't get candy bags at the Christmas program this year," she said, noticing them standing nearby like beggars, their eyes as wide as the Amazon. "I was glad the church used the money for something else, but…well, I thought your children should have something too."

As the kids stood there drooling, I reached for the bag and pulled out a box of chocolates and some candy canes. "They're all for me," I said. And after thanking Avonelle profusely, I ran to the bedroom, locked the door, and made munching sounds.

When you first meet Avonelle, her smile might throw you off a little. It seems to indicate that life has been kind to her. That her trunk has remained free of those furry little creatures with the stripe down their back. But while the storm of my wife's illness entered our home, threatening to blow paint off the walls, this woman's story stood out as a shining example of where to go when the worst becomes reality.

Her story was a gift she brought us.

Offered with a smile.

I unlocked the door and shared the chocolates with the kids. Let me share this story with you…

Light from the dashboard threw a pale glow on the haggard face of the aging man. Gripping the steering wheel, he peered into the night. *Let's see now,* he thought, wrinkling his brow, *how could it take me twelve hours to drive sixty miles?*

Earlier that day he'd driven south from Red Deer, Alberta, Canada, toward our small town, but somehow he'd taken a detour, ending up three hundred miles east in a neighboring province.

"You need to retrace your path," a stranger told him. "You need to turn around. And head west."

But the detour continued. Five hours later he arrived in Edmonton, a city far to the north, and now he was standing on the side of the road rubbing burning eyes in bewilderment. In his hand was a piece of paper with directions to another city far from home. Climbing back into the car, he turned up the radio. Someone was missing, possibly lost. Someone who was sick.

Twenty-four hours later, George Martin quit searching for home and pulled into a tiny service station in a town east of Edmonton. Exhausted, hungry and thirsty, he approached the woman behind the till. "I left my wife somewhere and I don't know where," George said through cracked and bloody lips. "But I have her sweater here."

When two of his children arrived to pick him up, George looked at his daughter Janis and said, "Oh, thank goodness, they've found you."

For thirty-six hours, search parties had scoured the country by land and air, looking for the retired garage foreman who'd driven away from the Red Deer Regional Hospital during some tests. Officials watched at border crossings. Radio and television stations aired the alert. Prayer chains formed.

And at home his wife waited.

Hoping.

Fearing the worst.

When George came through the door, she embraced him tightly. "Ah, honey," smiled Avonelle, "you took the long way home, didn't you?"

But George wasn't really home. As the poison of a dread disease began to spread through his body, he felt like a stranger in his own house, not knowing that Home waited too far down the road in a land not made with hands.

Years before the doctors diagnosed the problem, Avonelle had her suspicions. When he burned up the car's motor for lack of oil, she began to wonder. When he stood in a doctor's office, wondering what he was doing there, it began to dawn on her. One day he jumped suddenly to his feet and insisted on making a delivery— though he'd been retired for years.

And then she knew. George had Alzheimer's.

"It took me a long time to get the keys away from him," she remembers with a laugh. "I finally discovered that if I told him it was my turn to drive, he was fine with that."

For three and a half years Avonelle cared for him constantly at home. She watched his strong body shrivel into a skeleton. She read the stories of Alzheimer's wards. Places where dignified saints wear diapers and swear like sailors. Where families stand with tear-stained faces wondering at the strangers they once called Daddy. Or Mommy. Or sweetheart. Places where God-fearing partners clutch their sanity, clench their teeth, and walk away. For good.

But not Avonelle Martin.

"There was no other option," she says now. "Decades ago I vowed I'd be there for him whether he was sick or well. It wasn't always the easy thing to do, but it was always the right thing."

One day George made a visit to the hospital and never returned. Sick from exhaustion, Avonelle went home and for the first time in years had a good night's rest.

The next day she began a seven-year pilgrimage of daily visits to care for her man.

To hug and kiss him.

To sit on his lap and talk.

To take him out for walks and ice cream.

To feed him and change him.

She also grieved deeply. "I'd be thinking about George, about our early years together, and the memories would come back," she recalls. "I would break down and cry and cry." On one occasion, she stood in the rain outside the hospital and trembled under a load of despair.

"I thought, 'I just can't face this another day!' and I turned and ran back home and got in bed and pulled the covers over my head." She laughs about it now. "But after a couple of hours, I found myself going back up to the hospital. I walked in the same way I always did."

Like a magnet, her smile in the midst of turmoil drew other

patients to her. Doctors and nurses sought her advice. Her pain seemed to prepare a shoulder for others to cry on.

Four times she walked beside George through the valley of death, only to have him recover and defiantly live on. But at last, the withered shell of a man began to crack. Bed sores dug deep and turned gangrenous. Parkinson's disease curled him up stiff in a fetal position. Each heave of his chest became a gurgling fight for air. For three eternal weeks, Avonelle fed her dying husband with a dropper.

Then it was over.

On August 31, 1994, she said good night for the last time.

"The doctors said he must have had 'ministering angels,'" says Avonelle with a broad smile. "I'd like to think I was one of them."

Angels like Avonelle shine like stars in this dark night of me-ism, of selfish rights and easy divorce. Surprisingly, their marriage was not exactly engraved in custom nor cradled in the support of friends and family. "That's right," she admits with a grin, "we...well, we eloped! It was a little more common in those days." But the roots of her unusual courage and loyalty run deep. In a kindergarten Sunday school class, she received a small plaque with the words "Be Thou Faithful Unto Death." Though she didn't understand them, the words would become her life motto. At the age of twenty-one, for the first time, she believed that Jesus Christ was the Son of God, and she made a vow that would shape the rest of her life: "Lord, as long as I have breath, I'll be a missionary right where I'm at."

Neighborhood children became her mission field. And amazing things happened when Avonelle prayed. A Russian boy believed in Christ before his dad was deported. The three children next door became Christians. Then their atheist parents. And after fourteen years of marriage, George too gave his life to Jesus. Avonelle started Bible studies and later, as a church deaconess, she began visiting the sick and shut-ins.

Did she pray for George's healing? "Oh yes. But my main

prayer for George was: *Lord, he's in your hands. The timing of his life and death are Yours. Whatever You have in mind, I believe You love us both, so I trust You completely.* I guess I learned to commit it all to the Lord from the very beginning."

When Avonelle Martin shakes my hand most Sunday mornings, she puts both of them into it. It's the way she lives. Putting all she's got into everything she does. But when I think of Avonelle, I don't think of her warm handshake or her welcome smile. I think of a simple faith.

Herbert Butterfield once wrote: "Both in history and in life it is a phenomenon by no means rare to meet with comparatively unlettered people who seem to have struck profound spiritual depths…while there are many highly educated people of whom one feels that they are performing clever antics with their minds to cover a gaping hollowness that lies within."

"I am a simple person," agrees Avonelle. "Not simple-minded. But I have a childlike faith in God. I believe that if He said He'd do it, He will. And I just carry on with that. But I also want people to know that I'm no better than anyone else. That always seemed important to me—that I'm no better than anyone else."

TWELVE

DreamsonIce

*"The only cure for suffering is to face it head on,
grasp it round the neck, and use it."*
MARY CRAIG

Once upon a time there was a little boy named Sparky. At least that's what his classmates called him. He was given the nickname in honor of a comic strip horse named Sparkplug. Sparky hated the name. But name-calling was the least of his worries.

School was tough for Sparky. His favorite subjects were recess and lunch. He failed every single subject in eighth grade. High school was no better. He flunked algebra, English, Latin, and physics. In fact, to this day he holds the record for the lowest physics marks in his school. Sports weren't much of an improvement. He made the school's golf team, but his poor play ended up costing his team the championship.

Sparky was a loser when it came to friendships, too. No one seemed to notice him. He was astonished if a classmate said hello. Afraid of rejection, he never asked a girl out. Instead, he devoted himself to the one thing he really enjoyed: drawing cartoons. No one thought they were any good, but that didn't stop him. He practiced on binders and scribblers and by the time he was a senior in high school, he got up the nerve to submit some cartoons to the yearbook staff.

They were rejected.

After graduating from high school, Sparky wrote a letter to Walt Disney Studios inquiring about job opportunities. He received a form letter requesting samples of his artwork. The letter asked him to draw a funny cartoon of "a man repairing a clock by shoveling the springs and gears back inside it." Sparky drew the cartoon and mailed it off with his fingers crossed. He waited anxiously for a reply. Finally it came. Another form letter spelling out rejection.

Sparky was disappointed but not surprised. He had always been a loser. This was just one more loss. Looking in the mirror one day, he smiled with the realization that in a weird sort of way, his life was funny. Almost like a cartoon character. Then a thought hit him. Why not tell his own story? Why not draw cartoons of the misadventures of a little boy loser, a chronic underachiever? He had no idea where his idea would take him.

The boy who failed the eighth grade, the young artist whose work was rejected by his own yearbook, was Charles Monroe "Sparky" Schultz—creator of the "Peanuts" comic strip and the little boy whose kite never quite flies.

You know him as Charlie Brown.

If ever you find yourself in the Philippines, walking cautiously along one of Manila's crowded streets where garbage blows and children gaze at you with hollow eyes, you just may run into another "loser." One who fell a long way to get to the top.

Limping toward you is a man of forty-five, stocky and determined. As he approaches, you notice one of the children climbing out of a makeshift cardboard shack. He is filthy. In his hand is an empty Coke bottle, his only companion through the night. The boy is one of Manila's 30,000 street children. Notorious thieves, they are labeled as leeches on society. Moonlighters are contracted to shoot them on sight. The boy with the Coke bottle runs to greet the stocky stranger. Bending down, the man takes the child in his arms. For the first time in weeks the boy is safe. For the first time in weeks hollow eyes are replaced by a smile.

But what of the stranger with the limp?

What is his story?

How far has he come to get here?

Growing up in a small town in northern British Columbia, Canada, Ron Homenuke learned to skate in the shadow of the Rocky Mountains on a rink in his own backyard. Proud to be the nephew of someone who had played with the legendary Gordie Howe, Ron ate, breathed, and slept the game of ice hockey. As a teenager, he reached the summit of success for every Canadian dreamer: the Western Canada Major Junior Hockey League. His stocky frame caused opponents to cringe and his 100-mile-an-hour slap shot caused goalies to consider other occupations.

Back when I was a kid, Ron was one of my idols. I loved two-hour Friday night trips to watch him play. At the age of eighteen, he was one of the most promising junior prospects in Canada. He was big. He was tough. He was a winner. I wanted to be like Ron. In 1972, the Vancouver Canucks of the National Hockey League drafted him. Ron had hit the big times. His childhood dream had come true.

But something was missing.

At a party one night, a teammate's girlfriend told Ron, a notorious party animal, "I'm going to pray for you. Something wonderful is going to happen in your life."

Ron just grinned at her. And had another drink.

Before long another friend told Ron how she had given her life to Jesus Christ and experienced forgiveness and peace. Ron watched her life and soon decided to follow in her footsteps. He didn't know much about God yet. But he had heard that those who come to God get everything they could ever want. That Christianity was a sort of insurance policy against pain. It seemed to be true.

Ron had it all. A professional hockey career. A good marriage. Money. Fame. Success. But one day he began to pray for more. "God, please give me a deeper relationship with you."

He wondered how God would answer his prayer.

Early morning sun glinted off the snow-covered peaks of British Columbia's Selkirk Mountains as Ron and a group of five college students struggled to reach the icy top of the Kokanee Glacier. Ignoring the warning signs to stay clear of the area, they reached their goal. There at the summit they stood speechless, gazing out over glistening white ranges that stretched on forever. They were on top of the world. Then, like little children they began to whoop and holler, sliding down snow banks, revelling in their successful climb.

But the icy slopes were treacherous. As Ron led the others down, he carefully picked his way along, attempting to reach an outcropping of rocks that would provide a foothold for the risky descent.

Suddenly Ron lost his footing. And began to slide.

His friends stood frozen in their tracks as they watched him vanish over the lip of the glacier, falling to a certain death. Down below another group of students gazed in horror as he plummeted two thousand feet through the air, like a stuntman in a Hollywood blockbuster. Racing over jagged slippery rocks, they found him broken and battered. Finally someone located a weak and unsteady pulse. While some went for help, others took turns trying to keep him warm. An hour later a mountain helicopter carried Ron's limp body to a nearby hospital.

While he lay in a coma the word spread.

People began to pray for a miracle.

Three weeks passed. Finally, fifty pounds lighter, Ron opened his eyes and glanced around the room. As he listened to the news his face twisted in shock. "I cannot believe you are alive," said a doctor, then slowly broke the news. "You will never walk again."

As time passed, the professional hockey player found himself struggling to perform the most mundane duties. "Getting a fork to my mouth was a major operation," he remembers. "I had to learn to talk again. And I spent lots of time in the corridors trying to get my wheelchair to go straight. I kept going around in circles." Then came that first step on crutches. And the first push-up.

Throughout the ordeal, Ron's wife stayed by his side, coaxing him along, coaching him never to give up. As his family cheered, Ron progressed from wheelchair to walker. Thousands of people attended a benefit hockey game held in his honor. I was one of them. Someone sang "The Impossible Dream." I was a kid in elementary school. I sat in the huge arena, crying like a grown-up.

On Easter Sunday two years later, Ron threw away his cane.

In spite of the victories, however, Ron was living in defeat. His hockey career was over. And so was something he now treasured more than career. His wife, who had stayed by his side during the recovery, packed her bags and walked away.

"Only one thing was left," says Ron, "my Savior, Jesus, and His faithful love. He promised to never leave me nor forsake me. And

I hung onto Him now." Before long he found himself learning to laugh at life. "I laugh at the silly things I do. At the silly things we all do," says Ron. "You only need two things to be a missionary here. A good sense of humor, and no sense of smell."

The first day I talked with Ron Homenuke he was stumbling around a skating rink, clinging to the boards. A few kids pointed at him, laughing. Some still laugh. After all, he's a loser by most people's standards. He walks with a noticeable limp. He stammers when he speaks sometimes. And he still looks for the boards when he pulls on a pair of ice skates. But Ron will tell you in a heartbeat that he's learned more from failure than success. That he's grown closer to God from falling two thousand feet than from climbing to the top of the hockey world. And so while trophies rust and sports records fall, Ron says he's picking up a few trophies of God's grace. The trophies are children along the busy streets of Olongapo, Philippines. Kids who don't have anyone else to call "Dad." He holds them in his arms. He gives them a daily glass of milk. He administers first aid.

Ron lives the words of James:

> Pure and lasting religion in the sight of God our Father
> means that we must care for orphans and widows
> in their trouble. (1:27)

I wish you could hear him tell his story, because he punctuates the paragraphs with broad smiles and an infectious chuckle. You won't find his cartoons on the pages of your newspaper, but when I think of winners, I put Ron Homenuke and Charles "Sparky" Schultz in the same sentence.

They're both making kids smile.

Because they've learned that things seem to turn out best for those who make the best of the way things turn out.

That you can't have a mountain without valleys.

That you won't see a rainbow until you've seen a little rain.

NO PAIN,
NO GAIN.

McPHERSON © 1993 John McPherson/Dist. by Universal Press Syndicate

THIRTEEN

Laughter in the Valley

"If you're not allowed to laugh in heaven, I don't want to go there."
MARTIN LUTHER

W hen I was just a boy my mother told me, "Son, choose your friends as you would your books. Few, but good." I was six months old at the time, so I didn't have a clue what she meant. But as I got older I began to get the point. Just as life's joys are multiplied when shared with a friend, so the weight of life's burdens can be cut in half. One of those few but good friends in my life is Gord Robideau. He's crazier than a loon, and he needs a lot of help, so we have some things in common. When Gord brought home a collie puppy and named it Sabre, he hung up this sign:

WARNING! GUARD DOG!
SURVIVORS WILL BE PROSECUTED!

A nicer guy you're unlikely to find. A better looking, wealthier guy, perhaps. But not a nicer one. Gord is one of those rare people who asks you how you're doing, then sticks around for the answer. He puts his fingers on my faults without rubbing it in. Our friendship was forged around backyard barbeques and late night walks when I would pour out the contents of my troubled heart. Gord listened. I don't remember great words of wisdom, though there may have been some. I just remember that he walked with me.

When Gord and his wife Joanne began their own journey through the valley, I did my best to return the favor. That's what friends do. They know the best vitamin for friendship is B1.

The other day I asked Gord to write out a short story for me. A story of those valley days. "No problem," he said. Then he went home. And delegated it to his wife.

This is what Joanne wrote:

I stood at the finish line of the annual Diaper Derby with nervous excitement. My husband Gord and nine-month-old baby daughter Annie were at the starting line. As the announcer yelled, "Go!" I eagerly held out a fistful of Cheerios hoping to entice my daughter down the runway. Instead, she lay on her belly like a beached whale. She had no idea she was in a race, yet Gord was jumping wildly as though this were the Olympics.

Just as many Olympic athletes experience hardship and adversity along their road, so had we.

The road seemed so long at times that I honestly doubted we would ever be experiencing the joy of being parents at all.

Five years ago almost to the day of the Diaper Derby my world collapsed. I was four and a half months pregnant and anxiously awaiting my first ultrasound. For years we had longed for this baby. We had prayed for this baby.

Horror enveloped me as the doctor told me that our baby was dead. Gord and I held each other and wept the kind of tears that hold pain so deep you don't think you will ever feel joy again.

Believing God is good and that all things work together for good to those who love Him was much easier before we experienced the death of our unborn child. It has been a long journey of learning to trust God again. Of coming to the place of truly believing that He is good and trusting Him enough to accept whatever He brings into our lives. With that trust came the desire to pray for a second child.

Against the doctor's odds I stood at the finish line, nine months after a problem-free pregnancy, my heart racing as Annie pushed herself into a crawling position, smiled from ear-to-ear and headed towards me and the Cheerios. She left the other Diaper Derbians in the dust. At the finish line we gathered up our daughter in an explosion of joy and proudly accepted the miniature gold trophy.

Five years ago I couldn't imagine this day. We are now the reigning Diaper Derby Champs!

The victory symbolized a greater spiritual victory for Gord and me. We didn't stop running the race ourselves and we allowed God another opportunity to create a life through us. Are we sorry? Not for a moment. Not even a few days later when Annie threw our cordless phone in the bathtub.

Prouder parents you will never meet. "I guess hardship has a way of forcing you to your knees," Gord told me during one of our walks. "It's amazing how many people we've been able to help because of what we've been through."

Allow me to pull the shade on this section with three more

stories of people who have answered the bell with smiles on their faces when opportunity knocks.

A year ago I was diagnosed with Lou Gehrig's disease. The disease took away my ability to swallow properly, control my tongue, or speak clearly. To make things worse, I'd always loved sports, but now a disease would wipe out every muscle in my body. When the doctors told me, I said, "Okay, God, what are you going to do with me now?"

God seemed to answer immediately.

The phone started ringing. People asked if I would tell my story at their church, at school chapels, Sunday schools, Seattle Seahawk's chapels, colleges, concerts, and on television. A movie producer is making a movie about my life. Ironically, now that I can't talk properly, I'm asked to speak all the time!

People are sometimes surprised by my sense of humor. When they ask what is the worst thing about Lou Gehrig's disease I tell them: "It's my wife's driving! She has to take me everywhere."

I've discovered that living for what you *can* do, not thinking about what you *can't* do is the key. I can't dance, but I can still laugh. This challenge has forced me to invite the Lord out of the attic and into the master bedroom of my life every minute of every day.

KEVIN JONES, BOTHELL, WASHINGTON

Each Sunday prior to Christmas, my daughter and I watch a perfect family, complete with husband, wife, and 2.3 children, hang the greens and light the Advent wreath at church. I sit there fighting a lump in my throat. A dozen thoughts race through my mind: I wish my husband believed in God as I do. Sometimes I get so tired of praying and waiting and praying and waiting. I'm tired of being a "Sunday widow." Tired of the tension at home on Sunday mornings. I know it's wrong, but every once in a while I sit and count all the couples and think, *Why doesn't God DO something!*

After twenty years of being a solo Christian in my marriage I've come to the conclusion that God *is* doing something. He not only sees my situation, He knew about it long ago. What's more, I believe He custom-designed this situation expressly for me and my husband: that He might be glorified and I might be made more like Him.

The one thing that sustains me most is the knowledge that God knows what He's doing—and that He's not done doing it. After all, I didn't come to faith in Christ until I was twenty-three; maybe my husband won't be ready until he's fifty-three. Or even eighty-three. That's between him and God. It's my job to love him and pray for him. I take great comfort in knowing that the Lord knows those who are His (2 Timothy 2:19). I also have this hope: "No, he is being patient for your sake. He does not want anyone to perish, so he is giving more time for everyone to repent" (2 Peter 3:9).

I'm able to laugh best when I rest in God's sovereignty. Since He is in control, I don't have to fret and worry. I can relax and enjoy my husband just as he is. So, I've resolved that if it takes another forty years, I want them to be good years. Years of laughter and joy. I owe that to my husband, and I think it's what God wants as well. His joy is my strength. Yes, it's hard at times, but I can honestly say I am truly thankful for this "skunk" God has given me. It's made me who I am.

NANCY KENNEDY, FLORIDA

On a warm August night I was outside enjoying a cup of coffee on the deck of my second floor apartment in the retirement complex where I live. Suddenly I noticed a big burly man coming across the lawn. He seemed headed for the apartment below mine. Approaching the door, he began loudly demanding a drink of water.

At first I thought it might be one of my neighbor's children or grandchildren. Then I heard a scuffle and cries of help. I hurried downstairs and rang her doorbell.

"Are you okay?" I shouted.

"Yes, she's fine," the man replied.

I ran upstairs and called the apartment manager, then hurried out to my deck, leaned over the railing loudly proclaiming that I knew it was an intruder and help was on the way. There was silence and I heard the man walk out onto the deck below me.

I grabbed a heavy hanging flowerpot and waited.

He was looking for me, but he didn't think to look up. That's when I took the pot in both hands, lifted it high, aimed it carefully, and released it. The flowerpot hit him directly on the head. When the police arrived he was still a bit wobbly.

Needless to say I was named "The Flowerpot Lady" from that night on. I also made a new friend and discovered that my neighbor was a Christian too. We had both prayed desperately that night. I already knew that God uses cracked pots. But I found out that He can use flowerpots too.

TONI-MARIE NORMAN, RICHMOND, BRITISH COLUMBIA

© 1995 John McPherson/Dist. by Universal Press Syndicate

FALLING ROCK ZONE

McPHERSON

"We're in luck, Dave! I found my Triple-A card!"

SKUNKBUSTER SECRET #3

Courage is fear
that has said its prayers.

The morning after Ramona's first seizure I navigated a maze of hospital hallways carrying a few red roses, and quietly pushed open the door to Room 1204. Ramona's eyes were shut. Her face was pale, her lips cracked. I busied myself with a flower vase, then sat by the bed quietly—afraid. For her. For me. For the kids. She opened her eyes then. And smiled at me. "I guess I stared death in the face, didn't I?" she said softly. "It's not as bad as I thought."

"People are praying…a few prayed for you all night."

"I know," she said. "I can tell."

I bowed my head and prayed again. Out loud. Nothing in the room changed. But for a few moments fear seemed to relax its grip. From that day onward I began to sense a slow change within me. A holy numbness, I suppose. Something I have trouble explaining to this day. The Bible calls it peace. It comes along when least expected, leaving us to wonder if it would have come along at all if we knew no pain. Or if we would ever exercise faith without facing fear. Or really learn to trust without experiencing a little turbulence.

FOURTEEN

Daddy Is Awake

"There are moments when everything goes well;
don't be frightened, it won't last."
JULES RENARD

When I was a boy of eight or nine, my parents saw fit to give me a room of my very own far removed from the rest of the family, in a rather dark area at the south end of our house. I'm sure they thought they were doing me a big favor by putting me there. After all, a boy with some space of his own is a happy boy, a well-adjusted, confident child, ready to face the world. But parents can't be right about everything.

For a boy of eight or nine there was much to be afraid of in those days, even outside that shadowy room. My older brother David cared much about my well-being, and so he made sure I was aware of certain dangers that came along with living in the Great White North. For instance, icicles were a concern. A twenty-four pounder with a razor-sharp point could do significant damage to a third-grader's complexion if he slammed the door too hard and looked up on his way to school some January morning. It's not a pretty sight, a child pinned to a snowdrift in that manner.

And then there were the bears. Grizzly bears. According to my brother, a whole tribe of them lived just beyond the trees out back of our house. Big furry ones. If you stayed awake long enough you could hear them growling late at night. Sometimes their leader, Vicious Vince, would growl mournfully, a sure sign that the tribe had not eaten in a while. And that Vince's cavities were bothering him.

"What do they eat?" I asked, proving that the person who said there are no dumb questions had not made my acquaintance.

"Oh, they like nothing better than small boys…they start with the arms."

"How come I ain't heard of no one being eaten?"

"They don't leave any evidence. They even eat the bones. And no one wants to talk about it. Remember Tom, that freckled kid in your class last year?"

"Yeah."

"Well, where do you think he went?"

I didn't know, I had to admit, as my eyes grew wider. And each morning on my way to school, I shut the door carefully and tip-toed through those trees like a soldier behind enemy lines.

On the afternoon of the day I took up residency in my new room, we watched a film at school. It was called *Mary, Queen of Scots* and I suppose our teacher must have left the room after she wound up the projector, because the film was intended for a much more mature audience than third-graders.

It was the true story of a queen who was married at fifteen to a man with whom she never quite saw eye-to-eye, judging from the fact that she blew him up with gunpowder in a memorable scene midway through the movie. But the final frames were far more memorable. Sentenced to death, Mary had her head covered with a dark cloth. Standing over her with an axe, a rather muscular man severed that cloth from the rest of her then dumped it with great ceremony in a wooden box.

We watched all this in black-and-white which for some reason only heightened the terror. Black-and-white films spoke of history, of accuracy, of finality. Certain boys in our class seemed to enjoy the film immensely, and on the surface, I seemed to be one of them. But as we filed quietly from the film room that afternoon, I knew deep down in my stomach that I would not sleep a wink until I was a teenager. And after school, I asked a friend to walk home with me so I could show him my race car set.

That night after the lights dimmed, I lay in bed watching my wall for strange shadows and listening carefully for strange noises. Neither were hard to find. I could hear a man creeping down the hallway toward me, dragging an ax behind him. The floorboards creaked. The bears growled mournfully. I pulled the covers higher. It was tough knowing how high to pull them. Should you completely cover your head? Or would you rather be aware of what takes place during the final seconds of your life? The hooded creature above you. The ax swinging down. I wondered how long it took for an eight-year-old's life to flash before him.

Suddenly…the sound of footsteps. This was not my imagination.

My entire body froze stiff, every nerve ending on alert. The footsteps drew closer. Looming in the doorway was a shadow, one hand on its throat, the other thrashing wildly toward me. The shadow growled: "Aaaaahhh!"

I lay stiff, unable to move, clutching my tiny chest and gurgling.

My brother David stood in the doorway, laughing, as if a heart attack was the funniest thing he could imagine me having.

I slumped and lay still, my eyes wide open. David's smile began to wrinkle and he reached down to shake me. "You okay?" he asked, genuinely concerned.

I didn't move.

It was the only revenge I could think of.

❧

For some reason David seemed to treat me nicer after that. Brought me things. Gave me an underduck on the swingset without telling me I would never come down. And on the following Monday afternoon, I came home from school to find him eating a Snickers bar. He even offered me the last half.

That very same day Mother hung two plaques neatly beside my bed. They seemed to share a common theme and though I wasn't the sharpest knife in the drawer, I knew what the theme was.

The Lord is my light and my salvation—whom shall I fear?
The Lord is the stronghold of my life—
of whom shall I be afraid?...
When my enemies and my foes attack me,
they will stumble and fall.
PSALM 27:1–3

"So do not fear, for I am with you; do not be dismayed,
for I am your God. I will strengthen you and help you;
I will uphold you with my righteous right hand.
For I am the Lord, your God, who takes hold of your right hand
and says to you, Do not fear; I will help you."
ISAIAH 41:10, 13

I would love to tell you that I dealt with all my fears that day. That as I memorized those Scripture verses, thoughts of bears and axes and icicles melted into peace, and I began to snore…smiling. I would love to tell you that ever since then my life has been one long stretch of fearless living, marked by victory over the concerns that face us all.

The truth is, it would take three decades and an eight-year-old of my own to teach me why we have every reason to trust, and no need to fear.

"Daddy…"

It is midnight. A small girl in socked feet stands in our bedroom doorway silhouetted by the soft glow of a night-light. "Daddy…I'm scared."

It is the third time we've covered this territory tonight. I take her hand and pull back her covers. Beside her bed hang the same two verses that once framed mine.

"Rachael," I say, "did you go over your Bible verses?"

"Yup."

"And you counted sheep?"

"Yup."

"And you talked to the Shepherd?"

"Uh-huh."

"Hmm…well, I want to tell you a secret. Something I hope you'll never forget."

"What's that?"

"Well, you see…some people seem to need more sleep than others. And I'm one of those who doesn't sleep as much as you. Have you ever knocked on my door late at night and found me sleeping?"

"Um…nope."

"So if a burglar comes, I'll be awake, right?"

"Uh-huh."

"And if a monster ever comes to visit, he can find me just around the corner, can't he?"

"Uh-huh."

"Then go to sleep, Rachael…Daddy is awake."

I kiss her forehead then. And her nose. And her dimpled chin. "I love you, sweetheart."

"Love you too, Daddy."

A few minutes later I tiptoe from her room and climb into my own bed, resting ice-cold feet on the back of my wife's leg.

She sits straight up. "Italian dressing?" she says groggily, then lies back down. And I go to sleep with a very satisfied smile stuck to my face.

It's easy to rest in peace when you know that your Father is awake.

❧

SKUNKBUSTERS

Fear is the darkroom where negatives are developed.

•

"A good scare is worth more than good advice."

ED HOWE

•

Fear is like a baby. It grows when you nurse it.

•

BIG WISDOM FROM SMALL FRIES

1. You can't trust dogs to watch your food.
2. Puppies still have bad breath even after eating Tic Tacs.
3. If you want a kitten, start out by asking for a horse.
4. It's hard to unlearn a bad word.
5. It's easier to see the mistakes on someone else's paper.
6. Sometimes the best one in the play has the fewest lines.
7. Don't expect your friends to be as excited
   about your "100" as you are.
8. If a tree had apples last year, don't expect pears this year.
9. Ask why until you understand.
10. You can't hide a piece of broccoli in a glass of milk.

•

Why suffer in silence, when you can moan,
whimper, and complain?

•

The shortest distance between two people is a laugh.

VICTOR BORGE

•

My little sister was sent from heaven.
They must like it quiet up there.

•

Worry wastes today's time
cluttering up tomorrow's opportunities
with yesterday's troubles.

•

Fear imprisons. Faith frees.
Fear troubles. Faith triumphs.
Fear cowers. Faith empowers.
Fear disheartens. Faith encourages.
Fear darkens. Faith brightens.
Fear cripples. Faith heals.
Fear puts hopelessness at the center of life.
Faith puts fear at the feet of God.

•

When life knocks you to your knees, stay there.

•

Strong roots grow best in the dark.

FIFTEEN

Journey in to Trust

*"I know God won't give me anything I can't handle.
I just wish He wouldn't trust me so much."*
MOTHER TERESA (1910–1997)

There's nothing like turbulence to teach us about trust. I am writing this chapter strapped into a tiny seat moving approximately 500 miles an hour somewhere over the frozen Minnesota tundra in a plane built by the lowest bidder. Beneath us the ground is blanketed by snow. It's forty below zero. Even colder *outside* the plane.

The stewardess goes through the customary warning...

"Ladies and gentlemen, welcome aboard and thank you for choosing 50/50 Airlines. In the event of an emergency, an oxygen mask will automatically be released from the ceiling above you. When this happens, kindly quit screaming and give the mask a tug. In the event that your oxygen mask malfunctions, please share with the person next to you. And remember, the lunch we will serve shortly can be used as a flotation device."

Two amber symbols light up in front of me. Symbols that always make me smile. "No Smoking...Seat Belts." I'm glad I didn't see those signs when I was ten years old. I didn't need any more ideas about what to smoke.

MOM: "Philip, what would possess you to smoke a thing like that?"
ME: "Well, we were flying to Utah, Mom, and I saw this sign..."
MOM: "And will you do it again?"
ME: "No sir, ma'am. I burned my lips on the buckle."

The captain has turned off the "Fasten Seat Belt" sign now, so we are free to roam about the cabin. I'm staying put. "We're anticipating a smooth flight," the captain has told us—a sure sign that we are heading for a test ride through Hurricane Henry.

Sure enough, half an hour later I am hanging on by my white knuckles, wearing a ginger ale, and listening to the captain's apology: "Well...ladies and gentlemen, I guess we underestimated the strength of this storm front moving in. I'll just ease us on up to 35,000 feet...whoops...sorry there...wrong button."

The gentleman seated next to me is extra talkative, thanks to some liquid he keeps requesting. "I wuzh on a plane like this one lasht Augusht," he says, louder than he needs to. "And the engine jusht bursht into flames. Kaboom. Jusht like that." He turns to me with wide eyes, then hoists a plastic glass for a toast. I make a mental note: if we survive the crash, stay away from this guy. He's the kind you read about in *Reader's Digest*. He gets desperate, he starts eating people.

"So…what do you do?" asks my cannibal friend.

It's impossible for me to hide when this question is asked. Two minutes later he knows I'm a Christian. So he voices a question I have heard on a dozen airplanes: "If there's a God, why doesn't He do something about all the suffering? I sure would if I were Him."

"If you were God, the world would be in trouble, don't you think?"

He nods his head and laughs. "I'm Randy," he says, shaking my hand.

We are not so very different, Randy and I.

Every time I climb onto an airplane I am forced to come to grips with my need to be in charge. I keep hoping they'll look at my ticket and say, "Sir, you'll be seated next to the pilot today. Enjoy your flight." I would like that. I would pay twice the ticket price for the privilege of looking over the captain's shoulder and offering helpful suggestions. "You know, sir, I bet if you took us up to 45,000 feet we could just glide this thing in…"

Makes me think of another flight. One that happened 5,000 years ago. Just this morning in my hotel room I read the amazing story of the Israelites' flight from Egypt. They weren't in a Boeing 737 like I am, but there are definite similarities. Just like me, they wanted to look over God's shoulder. To be in charge. To sit beside the Pilot and offer helpful suggestions. "Well, yes, Moses did part the Red Sea last Wednesday, Lord, but what's he going to do with all these Amorites and Jebusites and Parasites today? He's no Charleton Heston. Besides, did You realize that we are almost out of onions?"

Like the rest of us, they found it easy to trust when God did something miraculous, when He was visibly present.

> When the people of Israel saw the mighty power that the LORD had displayed against the Egyptians, they feared the LORD and put their faith in him and his servant Moses. (Exodus 14:31)

"The LORD must hate us, bringing us here from Egypt to be slaughtered by these Amorites. How can we go on? Our scouts have demoralized us with their report. They say that the people of the land are taller and more powerful than we are, and that the walls of their towns rise high into the sky! They have even seen giants there." (Deuteronomy 1:27–28)

"Do not be terrified; do not be afraid of them. The LORD your God, who is going before you, will fight for you, as he did for you in Egypt, before your very eyes, and in the desert. There you saw how the LORD your God carried you, *as a father carries his son,* all the way you went until you reached this place" (Deuteronomy 1:29–31, NIV, italics mine).

Life-changing words those: "As a father carries his son…"

Could it be that God cares as much for me as I do for those precious children waiting back home?

Outside our window, the plane's wing seems unusually wobbly. But for reasons I can't properly explain, I am at peace. I tell Randy so, and he sips his coffee, then shakes his head. "I just don't see how you can trust a God who would let that stuff happen."

"Sometimes I'm not sure either. But we trust this airline when we buy a ticket. I've decided to trust God no matter what happens."

Randy looks out the window, studying the wing.

A story comes to mind. The old preacher Vance Havner used to tell it. An elderly lady was greatly disturbed by her troubles—both real and imaginary. Finally someone in her family advised her tactfully but firmly, "Grandma, we've done all we can for you. You'll have to trust God for the rest."

A look of complete despair spread across her face.

"Oh no!" she exclaimed. "Has it come to that?"

Mr. Havner said, "It always comes to that, so we might as well begin with that. God's Word tells us to bring every concern to the Lord. Since He offers to handle our problems, why not let Him?"

And so, strapped to an airplane, buffeted by turbulence that forces me to Him, I type this prayer:

Dear Lord,
I can't carry this burden alone. I need You. I've seen You do amazing things in the past. Things that teach me to trust You for what I haven't seen yet. I trust You to do what's best for my wife. And for my kids. I don't know what will happen tomorrow, but I would rather walk with You in the dark than go it alone in the light. You said You'd never leave. I'm counting on it like never before.

And I pray a quiet prayer for Randy. That he will learn to trust, too.

In his book, *Telling Secrets,* Frederick Buechner tells of a time when, parked by the roadside, terribly depressed and afraid about a daughter's illness and difficulties in his family, a car came out of nowhere with a license plate that bore the one word out of all the words in the dictionary that he needed most to see at that moment. The word was TRUST. "What do you call a moment like that?" writes Buechner. "Something to laugh off as the kind of joke life plays on us every once in a while? The word of God? I am willing to believe that maybe it was something of both, but for me it was an epiphany. The owner of the car turned out to be, as I'd suspected, a trust officer in a bank, and not long ago, having read an account I wrote of the incident somewhere, he found out where I lived and one afternoon brought me the license plate itself, which sits propped up on a bookshelf in my house to this day. It's rusty around the edges and a little battered, and it is also as holy a relic as I have ever seen."

Trust. I know all the theological definitions, but for me it is best discovered on roadsides and in airplanes. It is a quiet confidence that though my world is falling apart my heavenly Father loves me enough to pick me up and carry me.

When I am down. And when I'm up. Even at 35,000 feet.

SKUNKBUSTERS

In Canada we have an upstart airline called WestJet, which has become known for its friendly service and unconventional announcements. My daughter and I were bumping along on a flight recently when an attendant came across the speakers with the following: "Ladies and gentlemen, we do feature a smoking section on this flight. If you must smoke, please contact a member of the flight crew and we will escort you to the wing of the airplane." Here are a few other examples of pilots and airline attendants using humor to make a long and sometimes turbulent flight a little more bearable:

"Your seat cushions can be used for flotation, and in the event of an emergency water landing, you may keep them with our compliments."

"As we prepare for takeoff today, please make sure your tray tables and seat backs are fully upright in their most uncomfortable position."

"Folks, we have reached our cruising altitude now, so I am going to switch the seat belt sign off. Feel free to move about as you wish, but please stay inside the plane…it's a bit cold outside, and when you walk on the wings, it affects the flight pattern."

"Thank you for flying Delta Business Express. We hope you

enjoyed giving us the business as much as we enjoyed taking you for a ride."

"Any person caught smoking in the lavatories will be asked to leave the airplane immediately."

"As you exit the plane, please make sure to gather all of your belongings. Anything left behind will be distributed evenly among the flight attendants. Please do not leave children or spouses."

•

"The adventurous life is not one exempt from fear,
but on the contrary one that is lived in full knowledge of fears
of all kinds, one in which we go forward in spite of our fears."
PAUL TOURNIER (1898–1986)

•

The LORD is good.
When trouble comes, he is a strong refuge.
And he knows everyone who trusts in Him.
NAHUM 1:7

SIXTEEN

A Wing and a Bet

"God will either give you what you ask, or something far better."
ROBERT MURRAY MCCHEYNE (1813–1843)

Sometimes we come across a story that changes our outlook on life. Sometimes we find ourselves telling the story to our children, our friends, and complete strangers on airplanes. For me, the story you are about to read fits that description.

Bob Hunter, a Washington, D.C., businessman, had just become a Christian. Every Sunday he attended church. Every day he read his Bible. Never before had he felt so alive. And never before had he had so many questions.

One day Bob asked Doug Coe, a fellow Christian businessman who led the National Prayer Breakfast, "Do you really believe what the Bible says about moving mountains when we pray?"

"I sure do," replied Doug.

Shaking his head, Bob asked, "You mean to tell me that if I pray for a mountain to move, it will?"

"Let me put it this way," Doug replied. "I not only believe it, but I'll make you a bet. A five hundred dollar bet. Bob, what do you know about Africa?"

"Nothing."

"What do you think about when you think of Africa?"

"I think of monkeys swinging through trees."

"Then here's the bet. I want you to pray for forty-five days: 'God help Africa.' That's all you have to pray. But you can't miss a single day. At the end of forty-five days, you judge whether or not any mountain has moved. If you think one has, you pay me five hundred dollars. If you think one hasn't, you just tell me, and I'll pay you five hundred dollars, no questions asked."

Now Bob was an astute businessman and he rather liked the odds. So he shook his friend's hand and began a daily prayer: "God help Africa."

A few days later he found himself seated next to an elderly lady a dinner. She told him she lived in Uganda and ran an orphanage there. Bob began to pepper her with questions about Uganda. And about Africa.

"Why are you so interested in Africa?" she wanted to know.

With some embarrassment he explained, "You'll never believe this, but I made a bet with a good friend." He then proceeded to tell her of the bet and by the end of the evening she had extended an invitation to the young Christian. Would he return to Uganda with her to visit the orphanage?

He said he would.

In Uganda his heart was touched by the orphans. After returning to the States, he got a few friends together and bought toys and clothes and sent them back to Uganda. After they arrived, the woman at the orphanage called. "Mr. Hunter," she said, "the children are so grateful for what you did. Would you be able to come back?" He accepted the invitation and before long was off to Uganda again.

After a heartwarming ceremony the orphans had prepared for him, Bob received a phone call from the president of Uganda. He had heard about the gifts and called to thank him. And to extend an invitation to meet with him that afternoon.

Arriving for the appointment, Bob found the president rushing out of his office. "I'm sorry," he apologized. "Something has come up, but will you ride with me so we can get acquainted?"

Along the way, Bob looked out the window at the Ugandan countryside. Suddenly the car jolted to a halt. Out his window, Bob was surprised to see what appeared to be a stockyard; only this stockyard was not filled with cattle, but with men.

"What is going on here?" Bob asked the president.

"This is a political prison," replied the president. "These men are my political enemies."

Bob looked out the window again.

"But Mr. President," he said, "it's not right to have men living in such horrible conditions. You must let them go.

"But they are my political enemies; men who have tried to subvert my authority. I cannot let them go. That would be foolish."

"You have to let them go," Bob insisted.

A week after returning to the States, Bob received a phone call. It was the State Department asking him to come to a meeting with the undersecretary for African affairs. Rather puzzled over the purpose of such a meeting, Bob had little choice but to attend. At the meeting, the undersecretary for African affairs asked him, "Mr. Hunter, on behalf of the government of the United States, I want to thank you for what you have done in Uganda."

"Pardon me?" said Bob. "The U.S. government is thanking me for sending some toys to some orphans in Uganda?"

"No, Mr. Hunter. The president of Uganda recently released the political prisoners, which is something our government has been trying to get him to do for years. He told us after taking this action that he was doing it because of what you said to him."

"What I said to him?"

"Yes. What exactly did you say to him?"

After the State Department meeting, the president of Uganda called Bob over the phone, asking him to return to Uganda to help him form a new cabinet for his country.

"But Mr. President," he replied, "I don't know anything about your country or the people who would best serve in your government. I'm just an American businessman. How can I possibly help you choose a cabinet?"

"Mr. Hunter," came the reply, "I trust you. Please come."

And so Bob went. And did what he could to help the president select his new ministers. After that, a close friendship developed between Bob Hunter and the president of Uganda. The president now stays in Bob's home when visiting America.

After forty-five days of praying, "God help Africa," clearly God had answered. He had moved a mountain. And he had moved Bob.

There was only one drawback.

Bob Hunter owed his friend Doug Coe a check for five hundred dollars.

SEVENTEEN

A Tale of Two Kings

*"The remarkable thing about fearing God is
that when you fear God, you fear nothing else,
whereas if you do not fear God, you fear everything else."*
OSWALD CHAMBERS

Imagine this: You are the most famous and powerful monarch in your country's history. In a recent poll, your subjects have given you a 78 percent thumbs-up approval rating. A cast of thousands fulfills your every wish. Each decision you make, each command you give is flashed across the cover of *USA Today*, the *New York Times*, and sometimes the *National Enquirer*.

But lately the news has taken a turn for the worst. Lately the paparazzi have been chasing your motorcade like mice after cheese, squeezing their annoying flashbulbs in your weary face, to illustrate a story you wish were not true. A story you'd rather not see in print. One that proves the crack in your kingdom has become a gaping hole.

On the same cover as the headline "Aliens bring Elvis back to a Cleveland Wendy's," is the first element of truth the *National Enquirer* has printed in years: "King's kid covets crown." Sadly, it's true. Your third-born son wants your job and he has begun rallying the country behind him. If only the tabloids would print the rest of the story. The lies, the deceit, the treachery, and murder he has committed on his way up the ladder. But they won't. And now the child you once rocked on your knee has assembled an army to rock you to sleep.

"King escapes heat in Arizona desert," screams the morning paper.

"While kingdom crumbles, the king retreats to royal digs for caviar," accuses *The Star.*

With pen in hand, you sit in the scorching heat of an Arizona July, toying with the idea of writing a nasty letter to the editor. Your reputation is ruined. Your life is at stake. An ancient book catches your eye. You blow dust from the cover and open it in the middle. As you read, the shadow slowly vanishes from your face. You are not the first one to suffer like this. Someone else has walked in your shoes.

Three thousand years ago, King David faced this very situation head on. He was chased from Jerusalem, pursued across the dusty countryside by his own son, Absalom, who wanted his throne. And his head. When David sat down to write Psalm 63, most scholars agree that he had fled to the desert of Judah, one of the most desolate places on the face of the earth. But what came from his pen was a letter that stood in stark contrast to his surroundings and his situation. What came from his heart is a song which is still sung today. One which offers us four keys to dealing with the most barren desert experience of our lives.

Listen carefully to David's words:

O God, you are my God; I earnestly search for you.
My soul thirsts for you; my whole body longs for you,

in this parched and weary land where there is no water.

I have seen you in your sanctuary and gazed upon your
power and glory.

Your unfailing love is better to me than life itself; how I
praise you!

I will honor you as long as I live, lifting up my hands to
you in prayer.

You satisfy me more than the richest of foods. I will praise
you with songs of joy.

I lie awake thinking of you, meditating on you through
the night.

I think how much you have helped me; I sing for joy in
the shadow of your protecting wings.

I follow close behind you; your strong right hand holds
me securely.

But those plotting to destroy me will come to ruin. They
will go down into the depths of the earth.

They will die by the sword and become the food of jackals.

But the king will rejoice in God.

All who trust in him will praise him, while liars will be
silenced.

What a fabulous alternative to a letter to the editor. What a
sparkling example for future generations that the God of the moun-
taintop is still the God of the desert. In this psalm David offers four
ever-fresh truths that every Skunkbuster should memorize.

1. Skunkbusting is thirsty work.

If you've ever traveled through a dusty desert, you have
experienced thirst. If you've ever found a skunk in your
trunk, you have experienced the frustration of hard work:
specifically, scrubbing the trunk with tomato juice before
you list the car in the classifieds. David knew what it was
to be thirsty. But he did not quench his craving with

Gatorade. Or drown his sorrows in alcohol. In verses 1 and 2, David tells us where he turned: "O God, you are my God; I earnestly search for you. My soul thirsts for you; my whole body longs for you, in this parched and weary land where there is no water."

How about you? In the darkest of times, where do you turn? What are you really thirsting for today?

2. Skunkbusters know how to iron wrinkles.

Shortly after a young couple's honeymoon, they decided to dress up and eat out at a fancy restaurant. For the first time in her life, the bride plugged in an iron, unfurled an ironing board and attempted to press the trousers of her husband's brand new suit—a wedding gift from his mother. But as she applied the hot iron, she watched in horror as six inches of one pant leg went up in smoke.

The groom rushed in from the next room, sniffing the air. "Is everything all right?" he asked.

Bursting into tears, the bride explained what happened.

"Honey," her wise husband replied, "let's get down on our knees and thank God that my leg wasn't in those pants!"

In far worse circumstances, but with similar insight, David got down on his knees and prayed: "Your unfailing love is better to me than life itself; how I praise you! I will honor you as long as I live, lifting up my hands to you in prayer. You satisfy me more than the richest of foods. I will praise you with songs of joy."

When we turn to God in praise, the joy He gives has a way of ironing out the wrinkles.

3. Skunkbusters put Shirley MacLaine to shame.

More than a dozen years ago on a Malibu beach, Shirley turned to the ocean, stretched out her arms, and with conviction shouted, "I am God!" Thankfully she was incorrect or we'd all be in big trouble. But millions took her seriously. Since then, the New Age movement has gained popularity, espousing the benefits of everything from reincarnation to meditation to spanking your inner child. But the concept of meditation is anything but new. What Shirley and her followers encourage is a twisted form of what took place in that Judean desert three thousand years ago.

You see, David knew where to turn when darkness descended. Although he was one of the most powerful men alive, he knew his own weakness and his need of God's strength. So he began to meditate on the truths of Scripture. In verses 6 and 7 King David says, "I lie awake thinking of you, meditating on you through the night. I think how much you have helped me; I sing for joy in the shadow of your protecting wings."

Skunkbusters resist the urge to look down or only within. They know that true strength is found outside themselves, in God alone.

So they close their eyes. And look up.

4. Skunkbusters know who to trust.

It's not always easy knowing who to trust these days, is it? One February evening in the town of Harlow, Essex, an English homemaker by the name of Dora Wilson looked out her kitchen window and noticed a group of men loading her neighbor's priceless collection of Persian carpets into a moving van. Knowing that her neighbors were on vacation, Mrs. Wilson opened her window and shouted, "Hey, what are you doing?"

"We're taking them out to be cleaned, ma'am," one of the men replied while flashing a winning smile.

Mrs. Wilson found herself smiling back. She made a

quick decision to take advantage of the service these young men offered.

"Will you please take mine, too?" she asked.

The men were happy to.

You guessed it.

They were burglars.

In sharp contrast, David knew that God was entirely trustworthy. He knew history. He knew his own story. Once he had stood before Goliath with a giant problem. He may have trembled a little, we don't know. He may have trembled a lot. Certainly he prayed. Then he watched God guide his sling, proving a point that would be remembered for thousands of years: Anyone who def God has rocks in his head.

Perhaps David remembered that giant problem when he wrote ...follow close behind you, your strong right hand holds me securely. But those plotting to destroy me will come to ruin. They will go down into the depths of the earth. They will die by the sword and become the food of jackals. But the king will rejoice in God. All who trust in him will praise him, while liars will be silenced" (verses 8–11).

Chances are you aren't a king. But each of us is handed a golden opportunity when faced with a desert decision. What will it be for you? A letter to the editor? Or a glance Home? Your answer—if you'll pardon me one more pun—will make all the difference in the world... when you're faced with a royal pain.

EIGHTEEN

Hey! Look Who Won the Rat Race!

*"All you need for happiness is a good gun,
a good horse, and a good wife."*
DANIEL BOONE

I believe that one of the greatest hindrances to laughter in our day is life in the fast lane. As I travel and speak to men, the most common response to my question "How are you doing?" is "I'm busier than a centipede at a tap-dancing convention." We live in busy times. Standard golfing equipment now includes a cell phone. We have satellites to find our cars, beepers to find our remote controls, and pants that talk. I can't wait for the day that someone invents a gizmo that slows us down.

I know people whose idea of recreation is twenty minutes on a stair machine reading motivational books. Who believe that the fruit of the spirit is push, shove, and trample.

A friend of mine has this on his desk: "We the willing, led by the unknowing, are doing the impossible for the ungrateful. We have done so much for so long with so little we are now qualified to do anything with nothing."

I smile when I read that. It's a reminder that treadmill living leads to a rat's life. Treadmill living also leads to greater anxiety, fear, and depression.

In *Through the Looking Glass,* Alice (of Wonderland fame) says, "It takes all the running you can do to keep in the same place. If you want to get somewhere else, you must run at least twice as fast." But faster running causes us to miss the things that matter most.

Bill Gates, who makes $30 million dollars a day (roughly $30 million more than I) explained to *Time* magazine recently why he doesn't go to church. "Just in terms of allocation of time resources, religion is not very efficient. There's a lot more I could be doing on a Sunday morning."

I hate to admit it, but I've been just as guilty as Bill. Four years ago I was flat on my back. Burnt out. Finished. Caput. I'd been guilty of pursuing the things I did not have as a child, desperately wanting to give them to my kids. And so I worked long and hard. Weekends. Weekdays. Coffee breaks. Midnights. If I had a life verse at the time, it would have been Hezekiah 3:16: "A man's life consists of the abundance of his *positions.*"

Life had blown some frightening storms my way, but few have been worse than physical, mental, and spiritual exhaustion. The road back was long and hard. It helped when my kids tickled me. When Peter Sellers and the Three Stooges came into my living room and made me laugh until I fell off the couch. I can still remember one scene vividly. Inspector Clouseau, the star of the Pink Panther movies, bends over to pet a tiny little fuzzball of a dog. In his trademark accent, he asks the hotel clerk, "Does your dog bite?"

"No," responds the clerk.

The little dog snarls viciously and bites the startled inspector.

"I thought you said your dog does not bite," says Clousseau. The clerk is one step ahead of him. "That's not my dog," he says.

Laughter changed my perspective, but Matthew 6 literally changed my life. In fact, I underlined the following paragraphs from the Sermon on the Mount so often that I need a new Bible. Take a minute and read them carefully, will you?

> So I tell you, don't worry about everyday life—whether you have enough food, drink, and clothes. Doesn't life consist of more than food and clothing? Look at the birds. They don't need to plant or harvest or put food in barns because your heavenly Father feeds them. And you are far more valuable to him than they are. Can all your worries add a single moment to your life? Of course not.
>
> And why worry about your clothes? Look at the lilies and how they grow. They don't work or make their clothing, yet Solomon in all his glory was not dressed as beautifully as they are. And if God cares so wonderfully for flowers that are here today and gone tomorrow, won't he more surely care for you? You have so little faith!
>
> So don't worry about having enough food or drink or clothing. Why be like the pagans who are so deeply concerned about these things? Your heavenly Father already knows your needs, and he will give you all you need from day to day if you live for him and make the Kingdom of God your primary concern.
>
> So don't worry about tomorrow, for tomorrow will bring its own worries. Today's trouble is enough for today. (Matthew 6:25–34)

If, like me, you find yourself caught up in the rat race, soak yourself in those words. They are liberating. They are life-giving.

According to Jesus, worry is irrelevant, irreverant, and irresponsible.

It doesn't matter if you win the rat race. You're still a rat.

So loosen your tie, kick off your shoes, and read the following list of practical ways to climb off the treadmill. You may even want to pin it to your stair machine.

50 Ways to Leave Your Worry

1. Give thanks for the sunrise.
2. Stretch.
3. Try yodeling while brushing your teeth.
4. Be friends with positive people.
5. Doodle.
6. Take a deep breath right now.
7. Ask how big your present crisis will seem one year from now. Ten years from now.
8. Skip stones on the water.
9. Make shadow animals on the wall.
10. Practice saying "no" in front of a mirror.
11. Don't know all the answers today.
12. When you can, walk in the rain.
13. When you can, have a water fight.
14. Thank God for a friend's newer car.
15. Duplicate your face on a photocopier. Fax it to someone.
16. Praise others.
17. Listen to music with your eyes closed.
18. Build a paper airplane. Throw it.
19. Sing loudly in the car. Roll down the windows.
20. Say hello to strangers.

21. Give the thumbs-up to moving vans.
22. Listen more.
23. Sneeze louder.
24. Read good books more than once.
25. Give a spouse or child a backrub.
26. Get help with jobs you dislike.
27. When on airplanes remove your shoes. Be careful with this one.
28. Plant something each spring.
29. Talk to your kids.
30. Talk to your neighbors.
31. Talk to your plants.
32. Exercise.
33. Smile.
34. Rest this Sunday.
35. Learn a good clean joke.
36. Be grace full.
37. Play football with a roll of toilet paper.
38. Find a child and read Winnie the Pooh together.
39. Avoid negative people.
40. Buy a flower. Smell it before you give it away.
41. Sing in the shower. Use the soap for a microphone.
42. Read a poem.
43. Whistle hymns.
44. Tickle your kids.
45. Try something new.
46. Have an oldies night once a month.
47. Take a humor walk—don't come home until you've laughed about something.
48. Enjoy a good yawn.
49. Thank God for the sunset.
50. Get enough sleep.

NINETEEN

The Stuttering Servant

*"Bravery is the capacity to perform properly
even when scared half to death."*
GENERAL OMAR BRADLEY

Have you ever been asked to do something you did not want to do? Dumb question, right? Most of us don't jump up and down about an opportunity to shovel snow, dry dishes, or peel onions. But let me ask you this: What terrifies you the most? I mean really causes you to cower in caves and crack your knuckles? I'll tell you in a minute what does it for me. But before I do, I thought you'd be interested to know that according to one survey the top ten fears among humans come in this order:

1. Speaking to a group
2. Heights
3. Insects

4. Money problems
5. Deep water
6. Sickness
7. Death
8. Flying
9. Loneliness
10. Dogs

Guess which one terrifies me the most? You're right. All ten. But not in that order. I'd rather swat mosquitoes than die any day. But for much of my life my number one fear was number one on this list: speaking publicly.

Eight years ago the phone rang. I answered. "Phil, we would like you to speak to our high school graduating class," said a sweet voice from a nearby school. "You went to high school once, so we'd like you to speak next Friday, the night before graduation."

"Um…" I stammered, "I would rather crawl across molten metal in a loincloth." No, I didn't say that. But I did say, "Well…uh…let me think about it for a minute. There, I thought about it. I can't. I just get too nervous. My lips quiver. My knees knock. My liver hurts. I drool. But…um…thanks anyway. Please call me again. In about four hundred years."

The lady managed a polite laugh before hanging up.

I set the phone down, noticing that my knuckles were sweating. *I'm no preacher,* I thought.

Two years later, I was elated with the release of my first book, *Honey, I Dunked the Kids.* After the first copy arrived I took it home for an evening celebration. While feasting at the kitchen table I told Ramona how the pop group the Bee Gees became so popular. "They went into all the record stores in Australia and bought their own records," I said. "It started showing up on the pop charts so people started buying it. We should do that."

"There's a slight problem, honey," she said, "we don't have any money. Please pass the peas."

I looked around for the book, just to admire its cover. Jeffrey, who was going through his terrific threes at the time, had taken it behind the couch with him. By the time I arrived, he had edited my book by chewing off a corner.

That night I went to bed with three quarters of a book on my nightstand. "Thanks Lord," I prayed, holding Ramona's hand. "We dedicate this project to you. If you can use this little twelve-ounce, I mean nine-ounce missionary, I'd be grateful."

A week later the phone rang. "Mr. Callaway, I just finished reading your book." *Great*, I thought, *there are now two copies in circulation.* "We've got a women's group here at the church," she continued, "and we'd like you to come and make us laugh."

I didn't quite know how to respond. Ever since second grade when I stood in the corner under a pointed cap making faces at fellow classmates, I knew I could make people laugh. Perhaps when God handed out the spiritual gifts, He gave brightly wrapped packages to some. Packages with golden lettering on them, spelling out words like "Teacher," "Preacher," "Encourager," and "Ordained Plumber." Marvelous gifts, those. Then He came to mine. The box said "Warped Mind." I like to think He smiled. And the angels rejoiced.

I said yes that day to the lady on the phone. I believe I surprised us both. But that night I understood why. You see, I had been reading the Bible through in a year (sometimes I make it, sometimes I don't) and I'd just reached the book of Exodus. When Moses, later to be dubbed the Prince of Egypt, stood before a burning bush, he heard God's call and winced like a pauper. "Wait a minute, Lord," he said. "Not me. I stutter. My knees knock. I drool." And the Lord said, "That's okay. I can work with that."

And He did.

When I got up to speak to that gracious group of ladies, I remembered Moses and I smiled widely. Sure I was nervous. My lips quivered. My knees knocked. My liver hurt. I may have even drooled a little. But they laughed. And some of them cried. And I found myself thinking of what I wrote in the front of my Bible a few days before. It was simply this:

Moses stuttered.
Sarah laughed.
Jacob wrestled.
Abraham lied.
Rahab was a prostitute.
David liked rooftops.
Samson brought the house down.
Jonah was down in the mouth.
Jeremiah was depressed.
Peter was afraid of death.
Matthew worked for the IRS.
Lazarus was dead.
Paul was a murderer.
Zaccheus didn't measure up.
    I guess You can use me too, Lord.

Today, believe it or not, speaking to thousands of people a year is the most rewarding thing I get to do (apart from smooching my wife or tickling the kids). Not because I'm so wonderful. But because Christ's power is made perfect in weakness. Second Corinthians tells us so.

I haven't lived all that long, but it seems to me that God continually chooses the most underqualified to do His work. Perhaps it's because they find it easiest to remember Who deserves the credit.

How about you?

Is there something rewarding you're missing because of fear?

Author Bill Butterworth once told me a fabulous story. When he was in eighth grade, young Billy was a self-described delinquent. In fact, he waited until the very last day of metal shop class to start a project upon which his entire grade would rest (sound familiar?). The easiest project was a screwdriver, so you don't have to have the IQ of a football score to know which project Billy chose. After shoving a steel rod into the fire until it was red hot, Billy placed it on an anvil and smacked it with a mallet. Unfortunately, Billy's aim wasn't so good. Unfortunately, he flattened more than he bargained for. And there was no time to start over.

"It was the ugliest screwdriver you ever saw," Bill told me, "and I knew I was toast."

The next day the shop teacher called Billy to the front of the class and made an obviously sarcastic speech. Finally, the teacher concluded, "Gentlemen, it gives me great pleasure to present the award for Outstanding Metal Shop Project of the Year to Mr. Butterworth...*for his chisel.*"

Now I'm not sure if this teacher realized it, but one little boy learned a valuable lesson that day. Go with the flow. Go with your strengths. You see, too many of us are chisels, but we spend a lifetime thinking only of the areas in which we've screwed up. I've been guilty of that at times. But I'm learning to go with my strengths. To use my gift. I'm no preacher, but that's okay. Chances are you aren't either. But you can be a mother your children will never forget. A janitor who is remembered for his whistle. Or an ordained salesman.

Whatever it is, do something you can't imagine not doing.

And never forget Who gets the credit.

By the way, I accepted another invitation. As you'll see in the next chapter.

TWENTY

Commencement Address to the class of '99

"He charged nothing for his preaching, and it was worth it, too."
MARK TWAIN

Ladies and gentleman, distinguished guests, surprised parents, relieved professors, graduates, and anyone else who can't wait to get out of these tuxedos...please allow me a few moments of your valuable time.

If, twenty-five years ago, you would have suggested that Philip Callaway, the ill-groomed child chewing pink bubble gum near the back of the French 10 classroom, would be a good choice to one day address a distinguished and fine-looking group such as yourselves, you would likely have been burned at the stake. Or at least made to stand in the corner wearing a pointed cap. But time has a funny way of changing things. And changing people.

Two years from now, if all goes as planned, I hope to celebrate my fortieth birthday. For most of you teachers that seems young. For most of you graduates there is no discernable difference between a man of my age and your great-grandfather who left you nothing in his will. That's okay. I forgive you.

When I turned thirty, my eldest son said, "Wow, Dad, you're old!" I asked him to explain himself. "You have cracks in your face," he said. So I locked him in his room. He's still there. We feed him through the keyhole. Not really, but I wonder what words of wisdom he will have for me when I blow out forty candles.

One of the questions I love to ask people when they reach milestones like the one you've reached today is, "What have you learned so far?" The question takes most by surprise. One cowboy had no trouble with the answer though. He said he had learned seven things while ridin' the range:

1. Don't squat with your spurs on.
2. If you find yourself in a hole, the first thing to do is stop diggin'.
3. Never ask a barber if you need a haircut.
4. If you're ridin' ahead of the herd, take a look back every now and then to make sure it's still there.
5. Lettin' the cat outta the bag is a whole lot easier than puttin' it back in.
6. The quickest way to double your money is to fold it over and put it back in your pocket.
7. Generally, you ain't learnin' nothing when your jaw is a'flappin'.

He's one wise cowboy, ain't he?

Children are never short on words either. Here are ten things kids have learned. Ten statements that prove kids say the smartest things.

1. When your mom is mad at your dad, don't let her brush your hair.

2. Don't wear polka-dot underwear under white shorts.
3. It's only fun to play school when you're the teacher.
4. If your sister hits you, don't hit her back. They always catch the second person.
5. Never ask your three-year-old brother to hold a tomato.
6. School lunches stick to the wall.
7. Never hold a vacuum cleaner and a cat at the same time.
8. Don't sneeze when someone is cutting your hair.
9. Don't say "Last one there is a rotten egg!" unless you're absolutely sure there's a slow kid behind you.
10. No matter how hard you try, you can't baptize cats.

How about you? What have you learned so far? One of the wisest things you can do in life is ask older people for advice. You didn't ask for mine, but you're trapped in your suits, so I will dispense it anyway.

I'm discovering that most of life's biggest lessons are learned outside a classroom. That they are learned more than once. And the really important ones may need to be relearned on a daily basis.

I'll stick with the important ones today:

Life 101

I'm learning that some of the most successful people I know didn't have a clue what the future held on graduation day.

I'm learning that a good sense of humor is money in the bank. In life. On the job. In a marriage.

I'm learning that a good attitude can control situations you can't. That any bad experience can be a good one. It all depends on me.

I'm learning that those who build bridges are never short of friends, that sometimes friends keep quiet, that your best friends stab you in the front.

I'm learning to slow down more often and enjoy the trip. To eat more ice cream, and less bran.

I'm learning that you can do something in an instant, that will give you heartache for life.

I'm learning that bitterness and gossip accomplish nothing, but forgiveness and love accomplish everything.

I'm learning that it takes years to build trust, and seconds to destroy it.

I'm learning to always leave loved ones with loving words. It may be the last time I see them.

I'm learning that if I'm standing on the edge of a cliff, the best way forward is to back up. That you don't fail when you lose, you fail when you quit.

I'm learning that too many people spend a lifetime stealing time from those who love them the most. Trying to please the ones who care about them the least.

I'm learning that money is a lousy way of keeping score. That true success is not measured in cars, or homes, or bank accounts, but in relationships. With God first. The others will follow.

I'm learning that having enough money isn't nearly as much fun as I thought it would be when I didn't have any. That money buys less that you think. A house but not a home. Vacations but not peace. Sex but not love.

I'm learning that helping others is far more rewarding than helping myself. That those who laugh more worry less. That when I grow up I wanna be a kid.

I'm learning that you cannot make anyone love you. But you can work on being loveable.

I'm learning that degrees, credentials, and awards mean far less than I thought they would. That I'd rather be known as a good dad than a best-selling author any day.

I'm learning that buying chocolates for my wife is money well spent. But what she really wants is me.

I'm learning that I will never regret a moment spent reading the Bible or praying. Or a kind word. Or a day at the beach.

I'm learning that laughter and tears are nothing to be ashamed of. To celebrate the good things. And pray about the bad.

And I'm learning that the most important thing in the world is loving God. That everything good comes from that.

For most of you, forty seems a long way off. Believe me, it isn't. When you're sixteen, you're invincible. When you're forty, you're tired. If you have the energy, you pull out old yearbooks one night or maybe study your graduation picture. And you find yourself laughing at hairstyles and clothing and the kid in the back row with just the top of his head showing (what was his name?) and you start shaking your head because it seems like it all took place last Wednesday.

The boy standing near me in my graduation picture holding bunny ears behind the redheaded girl and grinning like a five-year-old kid was killed by a drunk driver a few years later.

A shy blond girl behind me died of cancer. She left behind two beautiful kids and a husband who loved her.

I wish I had talked to her on graduation day. I wish I had asked her what she had learned so far. If she were here today, I think she'd like my list. And the list from the little kids. And maybe the cowboy. I'm sure she'd agree that life is what happens when you are planning something else. And I think she'd tell us all that the future is frightening, so take God's hand. It's gonna be okay.

And she'd wish you His best.

Today.

Tomorrow.

And all the way Home.

I'm getting so old that all my friends in heaven will think
I didn't make it

SKUNKBUSTER SECRET #4

Laughter is ice cream on the pie of life.
It adds flavor and makes it easier to swallow.

On February 14, Ramona and I walked fearfully down a hospital hallway and into a tiny office. Two doctors with expressionless faces waited. One held an envelope. From it she removed a single sheet of paper we had waited ten months to see. A letter with our "future" on it. Holding it to the light, she said kindly, "Ramona, you have the normal gene…" A thousand things flashed through my mind. The Huntington's gene. The girl I love will be an invalid soon. My children have a 50/50 chance of the same. I sat in stunned silence. Then she said: "…which means you don't have Huntington's."

We stood to our feet. "You mean we don't have it?"

"You don't have it."

Unable to comprehend the news, we repeated the question three times. She repeated the answer. A burden we had carried for too many years slipped quickly from our shoulders. Hugging the doctors, we thanked them repeatedly, then hurried into the hallway, laughing like schoolchildren. That night, surrounded by best friends and a seafood dinner, we spoke of laughter—a gift that had come our way long before we entered that hallway. During ten months of uncertainty, in the aftermath of a hundred seizures, we had experienced joy that often seemed to break out in laughter, causing us to realize that laughter is better than Prozac. It is the smile of God on a troubled world.

TWENTY-ONE

Laughter 101

"I have no understanding of a long-faced Christian.
If God is anything, He must be joy."
JOE E. BROWN (1892–1973)

Did you know that the average child laughs two hundered times a day? That's what the experts tell us. It's amazing to think of, isn't it?—that there are experts in this field, I mean. But I suspect their claims are true. After all, children laugh about everything. A middle-aged man hopping about the yard yelling after hitting his thumb with a hammer is a very funny thing to a four-year-old. A thick rubber band shot at Daddy's newspaper and registering a loud thwaaack! after Daddy has endured a tough day of highly intense meetings in which he had to defend some declining sales figures, is just about the funniest thing that same four-year-old can imagine. He just may laugh about this for weeks.

And he's likely to try it again.

Just to hear Daddy holler.

Adults, on the other hand, don't laugh so well. In fact, those same experts tell us that we adults laugh an average of four times a day. Incredible, isn't it? (I think some of us laugh more than that, but remember your high school biology teacher? He balanced out the average.) Where did we lose 196 laughs a day?

A few months ago I was speaking to a thousand people in a church in beautiful British Columbia, Canada. My topic was "The Last Laugh." Surrounded by colorful stained-glass windows in a denomination known more for sobriety than smiles, I asked with a timid grin, "Do you think it's okay for us to laugh in here?"

Smiles broke out in every pew.

As I began recounting some of the hilarious things my children had said over the years, the smiles turned to laughter. "We had three kids in three years," I told them. "Someone asked me what that's like. I told him we're far more satisfied than the man who has three million dollars.

"How so?

"Well, the guy with three million wants more."

It took a second or two for some to catch on, but once they did, they laughed quite heartily. I went on to say that our children aren't always learning what we think they're learning in Sunday school. As proof, I submitted the following statements from Sunday school students. Actual quotes that have made teachers laugh and parents cry. Here are a few samples:

The first commandment was when Eve told Adam to eat the apple.
Solomon had 200 wives and 700 porcupines.
The people who followed Jesus were called the twelve oppossums.
The Golden Rule says to do one to others before they do one to you.
A Christian can have only one wife. This is called monotony.
Lot's wife was a pillar of salt by day and a ball of fire by night.

As I finished the last line, one dear lady struggled to her feet and shuffled through the back doors, giving an usher an earful on the way. "There's no place for that kind of thing in church," she told him. "You tell Mr. Callaway that."

What this dear lady missed was joining 999 others in celebrating our reason for laughter: The glorious hope of heaven. And the joy Christ can give His children on earth.

My friend and fellow comedian Ken Davis (whom I will continue to admire greatly until he beats me at golf) was speaking at a church one night. In the midst of his message he happened to notice in the front pew a gentleman who couldn't locate his funny bone if his life depended on it. Ken tried his best jokes (and believe me, they're good), but to no avail. The man sat stoically, frowning at Ken throughout his side-splitting monologue.

After the meeting, the man approached Ken, who was prepared for the worst. Thrusting forth his hand he said with sincerity, "I want to thank you, Mr. Davis. I haven't laughed that hard in a long time."

W. C. Fields once joked, "Smile first thing in the morning and get it over with." It seems this man took him seriously.

Oswald Chambers, the author of the bestselling devotional of all time, *My Utmost for His Highest,* was often criticized for his sense of humor. After meeting Oswald for the first time, a rather serious young man who didn't take much to smiling said, "I was shocked at what I then considered his undue levity. He was the most irreverent reverend I had ever met!"

While visiting a family in London, Oswald stayed home with the two children so their parents could attend a Sunday evening service. The couple was confident to leave the kids in the care of this great saint who traveled the country as a minister. Upon arriving home later that night, they tucked the children into bed. "Did Reverend Chambers teach you a nice song or Bible verse?" the mother asked.

"Oh, yes," said the children. "We'll say it." And they did. In perfect unison:

Little Willie in best of sashes
Fell in the fire and was burnt to ashes,
Later on the room grew chilly,
But no one cared to poke poor Willie.

Oswald's laugh could be heard echoing down the hall.

Billy Sunday seemed to agree with Oswald Chambers. He once said, "If you have no joy, there's a leak in your Christianity somewhere." I couldn't agree more. I believe in a holy and awesome God, the Maker of heaven and earth, the One who alone is worthy of my adoration and praise. But I also believe in a God who created the wiener dog and the duck-billed platypus. A God who laughs.

Of all people on the face of the earth, Christians have the greatest reason to laugh. Yet, I'm ashamed to say, some of us show up Sunday morning with our faces so puckered that we could suck buttons off a sofa. Here are ten simple exercises for sofa-suckers:

1. Glue a quarter to the sidewalk then watch what happens.
2. Make faces in a toaster.
3. Make faces in an elevator.
4. Order a cheeseburger with no cheese.
5. Make up a foreign language and ask for directions.
6. Walk up a flight of stairs. Backwards.
7. When you get home tonight, wear your pants backwards.
8. Pop popcorn with the lid off.
9. Read fewer newspapers and more psalms.
10. Place a mark on your body to show where you've had it up to.

If you are still frowning (or even if you aren't), allow me to give you three good reasons to laugh.

1. God's grace goes deeper than our deepest sin.

One of my author friends is Lee Strobel who has written several excellent books including *The Case for Christ*. In the summer of 1974, while I was slogging my way through seventh grade, Lee was an eager young journalist working at the *Chicago Tribune*. While I was pursuing a cute girl near the back of the classroom, Lee was pursuing fame, pleasure, and wealth. I came up empty. Lee didn't. Before long he had the world in his pocket. A law degree from prestigious Yale. Award-winning crime stories gracing the front pages. But four years later Lee's world began to unravel.

Central to his selfish pursuits had always been the belief that there was no God. To him the idea of a loving Creator was absurd. But when his wife came home from church one day with the news that she believed Jesus Christ was the Son of God, Lee stood dumbfounded. Over the months he watched her life. He thought Christianity would make her stuffy, boring, and dull. Instead her smile wouldn't go away. She was more fun than ever. Unable to deny the dramatic change in her, Lee decided to combine his legal training and journalistic savvy to systematically pick apart Christianity. Two years later his journey through the evidence took him to the same place it has taken millions of skeptics throughout history: the foot of the cross.

I talked to Lee recently, asking him for one good reason to laugh. Lee told me that he had read an article I had written in *Servant* magazine in which I talked about what I wanted on my tombstone. Alfred Hitchcock said he wanted his to say, "This is what they do to bad little boys," and someone else has as his epitaph, "Here lies an atheist, all dressed up and no place to go." But I wrote that I want mine to say, "He found God's grace too amazing to keep to himself."

Lee read that and stopped. Then he read the statement to his wife. "That's what I want on mine," he told her. Lee said, "I am so bowled over by the fact that God would forgive someone who led such a disgusting and immoral life for so many years. There is a daily sense of wonder that God has not only adopted me as a son, but given me a ministry reaching out to people like I once was. It overwhelms me."

God's grace should overwhelm all of us, shouldn't it? I know of no better reason in all the world to celebrate than this: We don't get what we deserve. We get something far better. It's called grace.

2.   The darkest clouds can't block the sun.

Another author whose writings I appreciate even more than Lee Strobel's (sorry Lee) is the apostle Paul. Talk about a guy who had every reason to frown. He left the power, pay, and popularity of a career as a respected religious hit-man to follow Christ. By earthly standards it didn't pay off. Five times he received thirty-nine lashes. Three times he was beaten with rods. Three times he was shipwrecked. Once he was stoned. Yet, left without food and thrown from prison to prison, the apostle Paul writes,

> Rejoice in the Lord always. I will say it again: Rejoice!
> (PHILIPPIANS 4:4, NIV)

Are you serious, Paul? Rejoice?

"Yes," Paul would say. "Don't worry about anything; instead, pray about everything. Tell God what you need, and thank him for all he has done. If you do this, you will experience God's peace" (Philippians 4:6–7).

But just a minute, sir. How do I rejoice when everything around me says *fear*? When the future says *worry*? When my circumstances say *pack it in*?

"Choose to do it," Paul would say. "Make a conscious decision to rejoice. For you see, joy does not overlook our circumstances. It overrides them." Paul provides a very practical key to joy in verse 8: "Think about things that are pure and lovely and admirable. Think about things that are excellent and worthy of praise." When we follow Paul's advice, a smile is bound to form on our faces, changing our countenance, our outlook, and bringing us joy.

3. The worst is yet to come. But so is the best.

Two eight-year-olds were talking after school one day. The one asked the other, "Wouldn't you hate to wear glasses all the time?"

The other responded, "Nope. Not if I had the kind Grandma wears. She sees how to fix lots of stuff, and she sees lots of cool things to do on rainy days, and she sees when folks are tired and sad, and what will make them feel better, and she always sees what you meant to do even if you haven't gotten things right just yet. I asked her one day how she could see that way, and she said it was the way she had learned to look at things when she got older. So it must be her glasses."

I love Grandma's way of looking at things, don't you? Perhaps it's because I am an eternal optimist. In the times in which we live, I don't see much use in being anything else. Yes, I believe that this world is a sin-cursed place. But I believe there is a cure. I believe that life will not be a smooth voyage. But one day I'll be Home for good. And sometimes I find myself smiling about that.

Listen to the perceptive words of Pat Willhoit, otherwise known as Dr. Isaac the Clown: "You can't laugh and be mad. You can't laugh and worry, because stress, worry, and laughter are not compatible. Laughter is low-calorie, caffeine-free, no sodium, no preservatives or additives; it's 100 percent natural and one size fits all. Laughter truly is God's gift. You can get high on laughter but never OD. Laughter is contagious; once it starts, little can be done to stop it. Laughter never felt bad, committed a crime, started a war, or broke up a relationship. Laughter is shared by the giver and receiver. Laughter costs nothing and is not taxable."

Could you use a good laugh today? You may not be able to muster up two hundred of them, but the people around you could use your smile, couldn't they? If you need something to laugh about, check out Skunkbusters.

And don't forget to try on Grandma's glasses.

SKUNKBUSTERS

Have you laughed yet today? Whether you have or not, try reading these actual quotes and quips out loud to a friend, a child, a spouse, or an unsuspecting fellow passenger in an airplane, bus, or elevator. They just may provide you with two hundred laughs today.

•

Classified ad: "An unexpected vacancy for a knife-thrower's assistant.
Rehearsals start immediately."

•

Newspaper ad: "Extremely independent male. 17 years old.
Needs to rent room. Call his mother at…"

•

Advertisement: "Try our cough syrup.
You will never get any better."

•

For Sale: Bull dog. Will eat anything. Loves small children.

•

Child to mother after school:
"Our new teacher taught us all about fossils.
Before she came to class I didn't know what a fossil looked like."

•

Child's definition of syntax:
"All the money collected at church from sinners."

•

Job seeker on application: "I have an obsession for detail.
I like to make sure I cross my i's and dot my t's."

•

A small town newspaper announcement:
"Gordie Jefferson celebrated his fifth birthday with a party for eight little fiends."

•

Elderly lady to a friend:
"I will just die if nobody comes to my funeral."

•

"Ninety percent of the game is half mental."
YOGI BERRA, ON BASEBALL, THE THINKING MAN'S GAME.

•

"I like long walks.
Especially if they are taken by people who annoy me."
FRED ALLEN

•

"I find television very educational.
When it's on I go into the other room and read a book."
GROUCHO MARX

•

"Basically my wife was immature.
I'd be at home in the bath and she'd come in and sink my boats."
WOODY ALLEN

•

And the real reason to laugh:
"Peace I leave with you; my peace I give you.
I do not give to you as the world gives.
Do not let your hearts be troubled and do not be afraid."
JOHN 14:27 (NIV)

•

"As far from the east is from the west.
so far has he removed our transgressions from us."
PSALM 103:12 (NIV)

TWENTY-TWO

Who Put the Frog in My Peas?

*"We all agree that forgiveness is a beautiful idea
until we have to practice it."*
C. S. LEWIS (1898–1963)

I have the flu. I think they call it The Shanghai Swine Flu. Symptoms include irritability, nausea, and the distinct feeling that a steamroller is driving over my funny bone.

I wasn't going to be sick this winter. Not me. I am in the prime of life. I exercise biweekly. I take my vitamins. But a few days ago we went to a certain taco joint and super-sized everything. After thanking God for those tacos, I polished off two of them which were piled thicker than the ring around Saturn with beans, beef, lettuce, tomatoes, pickles, beans, mustard, and—did I mention the beans? Six hours later, I was staring facedown into an empty ice cream bucket and wishing for all the world that those tacos were back in Mexico.

Ramona was awakened by the noise and came out to the kitchen. It is so good to have someone around when you're suffering like this. Someone who cares. Someone brimming with kindness and compassion. One who knows how to speak a soothing word or two. "When you're finished, would you clean up?" she said. And went back to bed.

The next morning the kids gathered around the sofa staring at the bucket.

"You sick, Dad?" they asked, as if I were a war veteran itching to tell my story.

"Children," I said, gently massaging my stomach, "your father is on his deathbed. Now I want to say a few things before I go. You be good to each other once I'm gone. Get to school on time. Take care of your mother. And don't forget to floss."

They just laughed at me.

"One other thing. If some guy comes around here hoping to marry your mother, you steal his car keys, okay? Can I count on you?"

Ramona came into the room, smiling widely. "Ah, honey," she said. "I'm so sorry you're feeling lousy. May I bring you another taco?"

"Children," I continued, "if this same guy should marry your mother, don't, under any circumstances, let him use my golf clubs."

"Not to worry," said Ramona, grinning even wider. "He's left-handed."

It's Saturday now. I'm flat on my back. The nausea is gone, but I'm still as comfortable as a porcupine in a balloon factory. "Food poisoning," was someone's diagnosis. "Consider a lawsuit," was someone's remedy. Perhaps I have grounds. I know I'm not alone. On page three of today's newspaper I read of Jackie Silver, a Sherbrooke, Nova Scotia woman, who isn't making her children eat their veggies anymore. Not after finding a dead frog mixed in with a bag of frozen peas.

Jackie was hoppin' mad, you might say.

The kids had eaten half the bag the previous night, before discovering the green spotted creature the size of a silver dollar. "It really didn't do anything to enhance dinner," Jackie told a reporter. "Most of [the kids] will only eat peas, so I don't know what I'm going to do now. I haven't had much of an appetite myself," she admits. "The sad thing is it's missing its legs, so I don't know if [they're] in the peas somewhere or if [they've] already been consumed. I didn't want to know for sure."

The story isn't quite what you're looking for when you're nursing a taco hangover, but it does get me thinking about some things. About frogs and the fairness of life. About the little things that can mess up our dinner. About the big things that can mess up our lives.

2

"Whatcha readin', Dad?" Stephen interrupts my thoughts. It's been an hour since I read him the frog story, and the child has been wandering about the house, a twelve-year-old with "bored" written all over him.

"It's a book called *The Sunflower*. Sit down. Let me read it to you."

I am halfway through, so before proceeding I fill him in on the pages gone by. Simon Wiesenthal is a Jewish prisoner in a Nazi concentration camp. Tortured and submitted to horrible evils, Simon begins to believe that God is on leave. That God must be away. And that He has no deputy.

One day as the Jews are being driven like cattle along a street in Lemberg, Poland, Simon notices a military cemetery. On each grave there is planted a sunflower, as straight as a soldier on parade. Simon stares spellbound. The flowers seem to absorb the sun's rays and draw them down into the darkness. Butterflies flutter from flower to flower. How he envies the dead soldiers. He will be buried in a mass grave like so many of his friends and family. No butterflies will dance on his tomb. No sunflower will bring light into his darkness.

Suddenly a plump Red Cross nurse approaches Simon. "Are you a Jew?" she asks. The answer is obvious. She instructs him to follow her and leads him to Lemberg High School where he once studied. The schoolbooks are gone now. Soldiers limp past on crutches. Wounded are brought in on stretchers. Finally the nurse takes Simon by the arm and pushes him through the door to what was once the dean's office.

The desk is gone. Cupboards that once held students' papers have vanished. There is only a bed holding a solitary figure wrapped in white from head to toe. "Please come nearer." says the figure, "I can't speak loudly." Hesitatingly Simon sits on the edge of the bed. "I am dying," says the man. "There is nobody in the world to help me and nobody to mourn my death. I am twenty-two."

Haunted by the crimes he has committed, the member of the dreaded SS begins to tell his story. The story of an idealistic young man turned murderer. The story of unspeakable atrocities committed against the Jewish people. Simon listens, unable to take his eyes off the man's bandages, unable to tear himself away.

As the story concludes, the truth begins to dawn on him. He knows why he has been summoned here.

"I cannot die without coming clean," says the Nazi, in an ever-weakening voice. "In the long nights while I have been waiting for death, time and time again I have longed to talk about it to a Jew and beg forgiveness. Only I didn't know whether there were any Jews left…. I know that what I am asking is almost too much for you but without your answer I cannot die in peace."

Without saying a word, Simon stands to his feet. And walks out the door.

2

Stephen looks at me with wide eyes as I finish the story. "What would you do, Stephen?"

He wrinkles his brow and remains silent. Finally he says, "I don't know…I don't know."

Out of the ashes of World War II comes another story. One which I decide to tell my son.

It is the story of Corrie ten Boom. Arrested for concealing Jews in her home, Corrie was sent to Ravensbruck concentration camp where she too experienced unspeakable cruelty. Her sister Betsie died. Everything she held dear was stripped from her. Everything but her faith in God.

Two years after the war, Corrie returned to Germany with a simple yet profound message: God forgives.

Corrie had just finished speaking in a church one night, when she saw a man in a gray overcoat working his way forward. "One moment I saw the overcoat," she said later, "the next, a blue uniform and a visored cap with its skull and crossbones."

As the former guard stood before her, his hand thrust out, painful memories came swirling back: The harshly-lit room. The pathetic pile of dresses on the floor. The shame of walking naked past this man.

"A fine message, fraulein!" he said. "How good it is to know that, as you say, all our sins are at the bottom of the sea. And God has put up a sign, 'No Fishing!'"

Corrie fumbled in her pocket, remembering his face and the leather crop swinging from his belt.

"You mentioned Ravensbruck in your talk," he continued. "I was a guard there. But since that time, I have become a Christian.

I know that God has forgiven me for the cruel things I did there, but I would like to hear it from your lips as well. Fraulein...will you forgive me?"

Corrie stood still, wrestling with the most difficult thing she would ever have to do. Her sister Betsie had died in Ravensbruck. Could this man erase her slow and terrible death? Then the thought came to her: Jesus Christ himself had died for this man. Am I going to ask for more?

"Lord Jesus," she prayed, "forgive me and help me to forgive him."

Still struggling, Corrie took his hand. Then the most incredible thing happened. "From my shoulder along my arm and through my hand," she wrote later, "a current seemed to pass from me to him, while into my heart sprang a love for this stranger that almost overwhelmed me. And so I discovered that...when Jesus tells us to love our enemies, He gives along with the command, the love itself."

When I finish the story, Stephen stands to leave. He doesn't know it, but the wrinkle on his face is gone.

I've been thinking a great deal about grace while flat on my back with food poisoning. And I've decided to forget the lawsuit. You see, I am not qualified to comment on Simon Wiesenthal's situation or his decision; I have not been herded like an animal down the street; nor have I witnessed the atrocities he has—atrocities that I pray will never be repeated. But I do know this: Like Corrie, I too have been offered what I do not deserve: amazing grace. And when I begin to understand how much I have been forgiven, I have no choice but to forgive.

You mean forgive my father? After all he did?
Yes.

You mean forgive a friend's betrayal? A spouse's abandonment?
Yes.
You mean forgive myself? Forgive God?
Yes. Because of the greatest story of them all.

Two thousand years ago one Man hung between time and eternity, between heaven and hell, bolted to a Roman cross. He had all the power in the universe at His disposal. He could have called down fire and judgment on His captors. But He didn't. Instead Jesus chose to utter these astonishing words: "Father, forgive them for they don't know what they're doing."

And so too must His followers.

When tacos go bad.

When frogs show up where they shouldn't.

When everything within us shouts, "Keep your mouth shut and walk out that door."

The forgiven must forgive. Those who demand mercy must show it.

I've told you my deathbed story. Allow me one more.

Many years ago the old Puritan saint, Thomas Hooker, lay dying. Several friends sat by his bed.

"Brother," said one, "you are going to receive your reward."

"No, no!" breathed Thomas. "I go to receive mercy!"

One day, so will we. I think we should practice up by passing it around. Down here.

"Nah, it's still not quite right. Put in more worms."

TWENTY-THREE

Letter in a Lunch Box

"They travel lightly whom God's grace carries."
THOMAS À KEMPIS (C. 1380–1471)

Two years ago we built a house. We were told not to. "It'll spell the end of your marriage," warned some. "It'll spell the end of your bank account," warned others. So far neither dire prediction has come true. But we are a SITCOM family (Single Income Three Children Oppressive Mortgage). I've always wanted to write something that would last forever, so I signed a mortgage. No need to feel sorry for us, though. We've been able to keep up with the payments by sending the kids door-to-door with a collection plate, and our marriage is stronger than ever, thanks to my YOBNOP strategy. Whatever my wife says, I respond, "You bet. No problem." It works wonders, this strategy.

Let me be accurate: one of the reasons both our marriage and bank account are still intact is that Ramona has never been one to ask for the moon—or in house-building terms, the Jacuzzi and stone fireplace. In fact, as it turned out, I was usually the one saying, "Honey, let's put a marble staircase here," and she would say, "Phil, have you looked at our checking account lately? We can't even afford marbles."

One of the small victories she allowed me was the placing of a French door in the pantry.* This, I reasoned, would not only look attractive when the bank manager showed up to repossess the house, it would give us the jump on children who like to hide in the pantry and scare us to death late at night.

I was glad for that French door.

Until last week.

Last week I attended a book signing in a nearby city. It is always an honor to attend such an event. Silver pen in hand, warm smile on your face, you sit behind a creatively decorated display table piled high with your books as adoring fans come by to ask questions like, "Um...excuse me, sir. Which way to the rest room?"

An hour after the start of the signing the manager assured me that my book signing had far exceeded her expectations. The last author (John Vaughn, *What Men Know for Sure about Women*), had sold only one copy, partly because the pages were blank. But I had sold eleven. I was feeling quite successful by the time I walked through our front door. And then I saw Ramona, standing in the kitchen wearing a strained expression, as if a toothache were driving her to extraction.

"What happened?" I asked, kicking off my shiny black shoes.

"Can I get you something, sweetie?" she said. "Some hot chocolate, perhaps? A piece of cheesecake?"

---

*Historical note: French doors were invented by Jean-Jacques Rousseau (1712–1778) who, legend has it, was trapped in a pantry for twelve hours when he was a six-year-old living in Paris. Upon his release he uttered the immortal words, "*Les portes devrait avoir fenetres,*" or, "These doors should have windows," a rallying cry during the French Revolution.

I leaned against the counter and took a deep breath. "All right," I said, "I'm ready. Hit me."

"He didn't mean to," she winced.

"Didn't mean to *what?*"

"Why don't you sit down, Phil? I'll get some extra-strength Tylenol."

"What happened?"

"It was an accident."

"*What* was an accident?"

"The pantry door."

There are times in life when I can still move quickly. This was one of those times. A split second later I stood before that pantry door. This morning when I had shut the door I noticed how nice it looked. Tonight the door had a jagged hole in the glass about the size of a little boy's Reebok.

"What happened?" I asked, my face wide-eyed and wrinkled.

"Well…he was doing dishes with his brother and he got mad. I guess he tried out a karate move he'd seen on TV. Go easy on him, Phil. He couldn't believe he did it. He's been pacing around in a panic ever since. In fact, he just went to sleep a few minutes ago. You should have heard his prayer: 'Dear God, help Daddy not to kill me.'"

I sat at the kitchen table then, staring out the window and pondering the events of the last twenty-four hours. That morning I'd been sitting at my computer when the phone rang. A friend was calling to tell me that an acquaintance of ours had died in the night of a brain aneurysm. He was my age. He left behind a beautiful wife and daughter.

"Dear God," I prayed. "I don't know what a day will bring. I don't know how long I'm here for. But thanks for this little reminder to keep things right with those I love."

Knowing I wouldn't see my son before I left for work in the morning, I tore a sheet from one of his scribblers and wrote a letter. This is what it said…

Dear Son,

So you thought I was gonna kill you, huh? Well, you're right. Meet me behind the woodshed after school. Bring a bow, an arrow, and an apple. I'm kidding, of course. And I hope you're smiling. Here are three things I want you to remember if ever you smash something again.

1. It's smashed now. No amount of screaming will fix it. But our actions do cost us sometimes and pantry doors must be fixed. So you'll have to help me big-time on this one. I've got some extra work for you to do around the yard. Your piggy bank will feel lighter, but so will your conscience. It sounds to me like you've already learned a great lesson about anger.

2. I will always love you. I can't think of one thing you could ever smash that would make me stop loving you. Except maybe my pantry door! Again, I'm kidding. But remember, that the age for getting your driver's license is now 29!

3. A house isn't as important as a home. A hundred years from now neither of us will care what our pantry door looked like, or the color of the car or the size of my wallet. But I'm praying every day that we'll be able to hang out in heaven together, laughing about times like these and celebrating God's grace.

I love you, Son.

Dad

P.S.: I'm glad your foot is okay!

I descended our plywood staircase, and prayed over our sleeping kids as I do almost every night. *The Lord bless you and keep you. The Lord make His face to shine upon you and be gracious unto you. The Lord turn His face toward you and give you peace. Amen.*

Upstairs, I placed the letter in my son's lunch box.

And went to bed.

The father of a SITCOM family.

With a smile on his face.

SKUNKBUSTERS

Poverty is hereditary. You get it from your children.

•

Better a lean agreement than a fat lawsuit.

•

Sign on an office door:
I can only please one person per day.
Today is not your day.
Tomorrow doesn't look good either.

•

"An archaeologist is the best husband a wife can have:
the older she gets, the more interesting she is."
AGATHA CHRISTIE

•

Kids Say the Wisest Things

1. If you want someone to listen to you, whisper it.
2. You can't be everyone's best friend.
3. All libraries smell the same.
4. Sometimes you have to take the test before you've finished studying.
5. Silence can be an answer.
6. Ask where things come from.
7. If you throw a ball at someone, they'll probably throw it back.
8. Don't nod on the phone.
9. Say grace.
10. The best place to be when you are sad is in Grandma's lap.

•

On a bulletin board in the Mayo Clinic:
Cancer is limited.
It cannot cripple love.
It cannot shatter hope.
It cannot corrode faith.
It cannot eat away peace.
It cannot destroy confidence.
It cannot kill friendship.
It cannot shut out memories.
It cannot silence courage.
It cannot invade the soul.
It cannot reduce eternal life.
It cannot quench the Spirit.
It cannot lessen the power of the resurrection.

TWENTY-FOUR

Celebrity Skunks

"Mountaintops inspire leaders, but valleys mature them."
F. PHILIP EVERSON

One of the greatest privileges I have had during the past ten years as a magazine editor is that of interviewing well-known Christians. After conducting more than one hundred interviews, several highlights come to mind. Sitting with Joni Eareckson Tada, who was strapped in a wheelchair, her eyes still twinkling with mischief. Talking with Tony Campolo, who is so busy that he's glad he has no hair to comb. Tony speaks about four hundred times a year, and he had just been on the phone to the White House, so I was well aware that our time together should be brief. Just to make sure I quoted him accurately, I kept a tape recorder running while we talked. Tony and I didn't see eye-to-eye on everything, and after about forty-five minutes, I looked down at the recorder and discovered to my complete horror that I'd pushed "play" not "record."

Nervously I told him the truth.

"That's okay," Tony assured me. "I forgot something once too. But I can't remember what it was. Let's do it again…better this time."

For the next few minutes I'd like you to meet some other gracious "celebrities." While slogging through difficult waters, I began asking these people to tell me the story of their own "skunks." And what they found worth celebrating in the toughest of times. I think you'll find their stories as fascinating and helpful as I did.

I first saw Gloria Gaither in concert when I was a seventh grader. Together with her husband Bill, she had already written some of this century's most cherished songs. Gloria loved to tell stories about her children and I would sit there, a seventh grader, fighting my emotions, desperately hoping no one in my class was around to see my tears. Last year Gloria told me the story behind the writing of one of my most favorite songs.

"Our family was going through a very distressing time. Bill had mono. His sister was going through a divorce, and I had just become pregnant quite unexpectedly. The Vietnam conflict was in full swing at the time, so a disillusioned generation was drowning its questions in drugs, and racism was tearing the country apart. Both Bill and I thought, *Who in their right minds would have another baby? What would this child face in fifteen years?*

"Someone very close to us stormed into our home one day and shouted at Bill, 'You're just a phony—you wouldn't believe this Jesus stuff if you didn't make a living at it!' This absolutely demolished Bill. But that summer when I gave birth to Benjamin, a perfect, precious baby boy, God confirmed a truth that had begun to push its way to the surface of our souls: It isn't because the world is stable that we have the courage to live our lives or start marriages or have children. The world has never been stable. We keep trusting and risk living because the resurrection of Jesus Christ is true. The whole principle is built into everything in our universe—life wins. No matter what—life wins!

"So we sat down and began to put words to what God was teaching us.

"When we brought Benji home, we hadn't solved the problem of what the world would be like when he grew up, but we wrote:

How sweet to hold our newborn baby.
And feel the pride and joy he gives.
But greater still the calm assurance
This child can face uncertain days because He lives.

"When Benjamin was in the turbulent adolescent years we often told him, 'Just hang in there, Son. We'll get through this. The song that has meant so much to people is your song. It's God's promise to you; He is making you into a man of God.'

"Many times since then as our children grew, our business life changed, our fortunes shifted, or our direction got cloudy, our family has found assurance in 'our song.' It has been a joy and somewhat of a surprise that this song, so personal to us, has been translated into almost every language on the globe."

Larry Crabb, a counselor and the author of more than a dozen books told me a story of an event that changed his life dramatically.

"Last March I was sitting in church when I felt a tap on the shoulder. 'You have an emergency phone call,' an elder whispered.

It was Dad. 'Bill [my older brother] has been in an accident,' he said. 'Phoebe just called from the airport. We don't know how bad it is, but she's really shaken up. Could you get down there?'

"When we arrived at the Denver Springs airport, people were everywhere. I stopped a uniformed airport official and asked him what happened. 'Flight 585 has crashed,' he said, 'There are no survivors.'

"I cried more tears during the next two weeks than I ever have before. One night I cried out to God: 'Lord, in this fickle world where you never know when a plane is going to crash, or a biopsy's going to be positive, when a husband or wife might leave, when a child might commit suicide, I know You're all that I have, but I don't know You well enough for You to be all that I need. And I've got to know You more than I've known You before.'

"I have since come to understand that there's something a whole lot more important than getting our wounds healed. We've got to find God."

When I first talked with Jim Bakker, leader of PTL, Heritage USA, and the Inspirational Network, I was the biggest skeptic. I have non-Christian friends for whom Bakker's much-publicized moral failures were one more excuse to reject the faith. So I was convinced I wouldn't run the interview. But his spirit floored me. He was a broken, humble, and soft-spoken man. When I asked him why God would allow someone like him to be broken, imprisoned, and bankrupt, he responded in a most surprising way:

"God allowed me to go to prison because He loves me. Those He loves He chastens. The Bible says that the trial of your faith is more precious than gold. I had been telling people that if they had problems it was because they had sin in their lives. I was teaching them how not to 'become gold.' It was God's grace that took me to jail. In prison, a young bank robber asked me, 'Why does God hate me?' When I told him of God's love, he wasn't impressed. But months later he told me, 'You're right. I'd be dead if God hadn't intervened in my life.'

"If I would have kept on going, I would have ended up in a mental institution or at least totally burnt out. I would not go back to the way things were for anything. God used the circumstances of losing PTL to bring me to a place of genuine brokenness, repentance, and surrender. It hurt. And the losses my family and I have endured have been many and irreplaceable. But in the light of eternity, it will be worth it all."

Former San Francisco Giant pitcher Dave Dravecky, who made an amazing comeback after a cancer operation, only to lose his pitching arm, seems to agree. "I've learned a lot during this ordeal," Dave told me. "I've learned how precious my wife and children are. I've learned how important it is to serve other people. Perhaps most of all, I've learned to put my life into God's hands. The hardest part has been the uncertainty. I had to learn to do what was within my grasp, one day at a time, and leave control of the rest trustingly to God. Such are the lessons that come when a man faces adversity. I don't think I could have gained them in any other way."

Most Christians have sung Twila Paris's hymns "He Is Exalted," and "We Will Glorify," but few know that Twila's husband Jack has Epstein-Barr virus—a disease that leaves him incapable of performing even simple tasks. Says Twila, "When Jack was too ill to continue touring with me I felt really alone. There were some dark times when the last thing I wanted to do was walk out on a stage and sing, but it has forced me to grow up in some ways I didn't want to grow. I am coming to the place now where I am able to say, 'I wouldn't have chosen this for myself, but you are in control, God. You are sovereign. And if this trial never lifts I will love you, submit to you, embrace what you have for me, and learn from it.'

"Many of us North Americans simply refuse to suffer. We will not put up with it! But Scripture teaches that suffering is a critical part of a growing Christian life, and that if we embrace God's will in our lives, the fruit of suffering is glorious. Christ himself had to suffer unspeakably in order to be the atoning sacrifice for our sins."

Elisabeth Elliot, whose husband Jim Elliot (famous for the words "He is no fool who gives what he cannot keep to gain what he cannot lose") was martyred by Auca Indians, loves a good laugh. During the course of our interview she mentioned aging. I told her about the three elderly ladies who appeared in court together. Each had been accusing the others of the trouble they were having in the apartment building where they lived. The judge, with Solomon-like wisdom decreed, "All right, ladies, I'll hear the oldest first." The case was closed for lack of evidence. Elisabeth Elliot laughed and told me a little about the trials and joys of growing older:

"George MacDonald said, 'If you knew what God knows about death you would clap your listless hands.' But instead I find old people in America just buying this whole youth obsession. You've seen the old ladies wearing sweatsuits and gym shoes, going down to the gym to work out, dying their hair, having their faces lifted and all that kind of stuff. And you know no woman is supposed to mention her age. Well, I don't mind telling you that I'm seventy-two. I'd rather tell you that than have you think I'm eighty. Who do we think we're kidding anyway? We all look pretty much our age. I think growing older is a wonderful privilege. I want to learn to glorify God in every stage of my life. Now as an old woman, I don't pretend that I am middle-aged or young. I am old and I am grateful for the privilege."

2

When Barbara Johnson discovered that her son Larry was homosexual, angry words were exchanged and her son left home, eventually changing his name, disowning the family, and disappearing into a gay lifestyle. Six years would pass before he made his way back home. She had already lost one son in Vietnam, and another in Alaska—the victim of a drunk driver.

"It's always darkest just before it goes totally black," she told me, laughing. "I felt like an elephant was sitting on my chest. My teeth itched. I didn't think there was any way I could possibly get through all the losses. It is a monstrous myth that faith in God is an insurance policy against the blows of life. Tragedies happen every day and Christians are not immune."

Barbara climbed in the car one day, with suicide on her mind. "I couldn't believe I had reached that point. And suddenly I realized that I might not be successful in my suicide attempt and could end up making baskets in the home for the bewildered. 'Lord,' I said, 'I can't handle this anymore. If he never comes home again, whatever happens, I'm giving my son to You.'

"When I said, 'Whatever, Lord,' I felt a complete sense of relief.

"From then on the Lord gave me joy. When we relinquish our burdens to God, He offers us joy and growth as we travel over the bumps and washouts of life. Not always in a limo—sometimes in a pickup truck, a bicycle, or even a wheelchair. No matter. The important thing is to become aware of God's care for us in even the smallest ways so that we may have abundant joy."

I've reserved the final spot for one of my favorite "skunk stories" from one of my favorite authors. A few years ago Philip Yancey told me this story of finding God's love in the most unexpected place:

"One holiday I visited my mother who lives seven hundred miles away. She took a box of old photos down from a closet and there was a picture of me as a child. I asked her why it was damaged. She said that when I was ten months old my father contracted spinal lumbar polio. He died three months later, just after my first birthday. My father was paralyzed when he was twenty-four. His muscles were so weak that he had to live inside a large steel cylinder. Whenever mother visited him she sat where he could see her in a mirror someone had bolted to the side of this iron lung. My father had asked for pictures of her and my brother and me, so Mother jammed the pictures in between some metal knobs. My baby picture was one of them.

"I've often thought about that. It seemed odd to think that someone I didn't remember cared about me. He spent his waking hours staring at my picture, praying for me, loving me. That crumpled photo is one of the few links connecting me to the stranger who was my father. The emotions I felt when my mother showed me that picture were the same emotions I felt one February night when I first believed in a God of love. Someone is watching over me. Someone who loves me. It was such a feeling of wild hope that it seemed fully worth risking my life on."

SKUNKBUSTER SECRET #5

Laughter sure beats Prozac,
but there's no medicine quite like hope.

I love playing sports. But I'm not a big fan of exercise. Because my wife loves me and would rather not see me taking up too much sofa space, she has developed ingenious ways of coaxing me to exercise. For instance, if you see me out jogging, chances are that she drove me out of town a few miles and dropped me off. I'm jogging to get home. For my birthday she gave me a six-month pass to an exercise facility. If I do not use the pass at least twice a week, I'm wasting money. I am a cheapskate. I go twice a week.

During a recent visit I found myself sweating aboard a stair machine and reading a tattered old January 1994 copy of *Details* magazine. One headline intrigued me: "15 Reasons to Be Hopeful about the Future." Here is a sampling of the reasons: Dr. Death is still alive (speaking of "suicide doctor" Jack Kevorkian); a Democratic president equals a swinging '90s (need I comment?); love lives in Hollywood (the writer listed five celebrity marriages—four have since ended).

In a church not long ago, I read the *Details* list then asked the congregation what gives them reason for hope at the dawn of a new millenium. The answers came fast: "God is in control," shouted someone near the back. "Heaven," said a dear elderly lady in a wheelchair. "God loves me," said a shy girl down front.

"Hope," claims one American cardiologist, "is the medicine I use more than any other." When I find myself sweating as I stand on the edge of the future, I like to think of a bumper sticker I once saw: "I've read the last chapter. The good guys win." The future, I believe, is as bright as the size of our hope.

TWENTY-FIVE

Tales of Mischief

*"The best way to keep children home is to make
the home atmosphere pleasant—and let the air out of their tires."*
DOROTHY PARKER

Tonight, after scolding the boys for feeding birthday candles to a neighbor's dog, I chase them to bed snackless, then sit in the living room, wondering if there's any hope at all for my descendants. "Do you ever wonder," I ask Ramona, "what will happen to a generation that doesn't even know which way to wear their hats? A generation raised on Nintendo and microwave hot dogs? I mean, seriously…sometimes I wonder what the world will be like when all the prayer warriors are gone. When all the great preachers and writers and missionaries have passed off the scene."

"I sometimes worry about the kids," admits my wife. "Because, well, honey, they're a lot like you."

Thankfully the phone interrupts our conversation.

The caller is a friend I haven't seen in years. Would I care to join him and a few others for a friendly game of floor hockey? Now, please understand that at my age (38), when you are just grateful for the strength to rise unaided from the sofa and waddle to the kitchen for six square meals a day, one should not entertain thoughts of dashing up and down the gym floor trying to prove himself a teenager. But there's no way I'm admitting it. Quicker than you can say cardiac arrest, I say yes.

By the end of round one my face is roughly the color of a ripe plum. "I think I pulled some fat," I tell my teammates. By the end of round two I have contracted a respiratory problem and, unable to find an oxygen tent, I suggest that we retire to my house for a healthy snack, namely Pepsi and chips. The suggestion is welcomed by Dave Wall and Pete Rashleigh, two childhood buddies, and soon we're sitting around the table swapping tales of mischief and laughing until my respiratory problems return.

The three of us grew up in a conservative community where we worked hard to make a name for ourselves. Unfortunately, the names some grown-ups called us are not safe to print. Here is a short list of our exploits to help you understand why (please do not let your children see these):

1. Using dark felt pens to add a single consonant to garage sale signs so that they read "Garbage Sale."
2. Sneaking into the church nursery and placing Limburger cheese in diapers.
3. Calling the morgue to inform them that Mr. Amstutz, our tenth grade math teacher, was dead.

We also tell tales of Super-Gluing salt shakers to restaurant tables, of signing classmates up for the military, and the strategic placement of outhouses, whoopee cushions, shaving cream, and Saran Wrap. An hour later the Pepsi is gone, but the stories keep coming.

"Most of the stuff we did you couldn't put in print," admits Dave. "My teachers hated me. Every time I turned around they spanked me. You check the dictionary for 'brat' and you'll find my high school picture."

Pete's list of accomplishments rivaled Dave's. "I was chased by security guards, banned from talent shows, and kicked out of Bible college…and that was during one of my better weeks," he says. "I used to steal tapes from Christian record stores."

The clock slips past midnight before we grow quiet…and a little more serious. Pete shakes his head. "On countless nights my parents lay awake wondering when the police would call. And praying for the day I'd come home."

Dave nods his head. "Same here."

On Pete's twentieth birthday, God got his attention. "I was going eighty miles an hour on a motorcycle when we crashed," he says. "I was lying in the ditch unconscious and I had this dream where everything was pitch black. When I woke up this guy was standing over me, his lips moving rapidly. He was praying. That was the day I gave up running. And came Home for good."

Today Pete is senior pastor of a Baptist church. He just named his firstborn daughter Karis—Greek for grace. And Dave? Well, he's quit taunting his teachers, and joined them. When he isn't playing practical jokes on the natives, he teaches the Bible to a remote tribe in Papua, New Guinea.

Pete and Dave know a few things for sure. They know that God has a great sense of humor, that He loves nothing more than watching wandering boys come Home, and they'd tell you anytime that their lives have never been more exciting than they are right now.

The clock is moving toward one as I bid them good night. The children are asleep, so I slip silently into their rooms, place a soft hand on their heads, and pray. *"Dear God, thank You that there is hope, after all. That You delight in changing people. Will You do as much for my kids? Will You take their energy, and shape it for good?*

May they find in me something worth imitating. And may they find in You everything they'll ever need to make a mark on this old world."

On the way to bed, I switch off the kitchen light and pull aside a curtain. Sure enough. Pete and Dave are still parked in the driveway, the hood up.

I guess they haven't found the potato I put in their exhaust pipe.

"Wow! That was neat! OK, now try it on high!"

TWENTY-SIX

The Gospel According to Matt

"I have to die this year."
MILDRED WARNER-BLAKE, ELDERLY LADY
WHO HAD HER TOMBSTONE PRE ENGRAVED WITH "19—"

I t is May of 1999. And I've been thinking about the end of the world a lot lately. Partly because I forgot my wife's birthday again, but mainly because I have a dozen books on my desk warning me that at the stroke of midnight on January 1, 2000, the world's computers will say, "We have had enough, Earthlings! We are going on strike!" And the entire globe will erupt in one gigantic cheer because, let's face it, we are tired of seeing Bill Gates's picture on the cover of *Time* magazine. We are also tired of those annoying beepers, those cell phones, and bank machines.

The downside is that the New Dark Ages will begin, in which there will be no electricity, no televised sporting events, and no microwave popcorn. To complicate things even further, it may bring about the end of civilization as we know it.

For some people, the end of the world couldn't come soon enough.

Take Matt Johnson, for instance. Matt is an acquaintance of mine who gets up each morning hoping Armageddon is no longer just a movie. He likes nothing more than a steady diet of books like *2000 Reasons Christ Will Return in 1985* and its sequel *1 Reason I Am No Longer a Prophet*. Matt likes nothing better than a good end-times debate and he can converse fluently about the latest pre-, post-, or mid-tribulation Rapture theory at the drop of a commentary.

Lately Matt has taken to reading end-times conspiracy novels and anything with Y2K in the title. I used to understand most of what Matt said, but now he uses words like "readiness" and "compliance solutions" and "Hey, let's get together and panic!" Sometimes he stops by the house to remind me which appliances won't work come January. My fridge, for instance—a perfectly good General Electric which my grandmother left me in her will—may have a computer chip in it, so digging a hole in the ground to store frozen hamburgers would be a wise decision. Among the items I should purchase "just to be safe" are:

- An emergency power generator ($399, batteries not included).
- Noah's Ark Grain Mill. Grind your own grain into flour (white, whole wheat, Italian) or if the whole thing is a hoax, you can still use it to make pasta ($429, includes shipping and ten pounds of barley).
- AM/FM Solar Windup Radio. Sixty turns of the handle and this puppy is fully energized. Guaranteed until the year 3,000. Retail price is $9,000. For you: $99.95 (includes headphones).
- Disposal fees. Ship us all your obsolete appliances (stoves, furnaces, computers, cars) and we will dispose of them properly for only $4,000.

I ask Matt if he isn't taking this a little too far, leaping off the high dive before checking the water, but he just points at my gas fireplace. "That'll be an antique before long," he says. "That's the only reason I'd keep it. It'll be worth something to a collector one day."

I tell him that I think it's wise to set aside a few things just in case, but that we need to trust God for the future. "It could be a great time for Christians to help others," I say.

But he just looks at me and shakes his head. "You are one mixed-up puppy," he says.

I was planting a tree in the backyard last Saturday when my cordless phone rang. "Phil," said Matt in a rather unsteady voice, "what I am about to tell you is top secret…meant for your ears only…are you sitting down?"

"I am now, Matt," I said, "Is this about Amway?"

"That was last month, Phil. Now listen up." Matt's voice was a barely discernable whisper. "Do you believe in the end of the world?"

"Hey," I said, "I live in Canada, I can see it from here."

"I am deadly serious," Matt rebuked me. "One hour ago I finished reading the book of 2 Peter. Since then things are falling into place. You see, I knew that the book talks about the end of the world. About Christ coming like a thief. About God setting the heavens on fire. About the elements melting with a fervent heat. But I didn't realize until today that if you take a Greek letter from every 666th word of 2 Peter, you can spell 'Microsoft' backwards."

"You're kidding," I said.

"No, I am not. And it gets even better, Phil. You see, the book starts on page 1,939 of *The Musicians' Amplified Devotional Bible*. And you know what happened in the year 1939, don't you?"

"Um…Hal Lindsay was born?"

"No, Phil. Work with me here. Hitler invaded Poland. World War II began."

"Where are you going with this?"

"Well," said Matt, pausing only momentarily, "2 Peter is the sixty-first book in the Bible, and if you add 1939 and 61 together you get—"

"2000!" I interrupted.

"That's right. Clearly it's the beginning of the end. The end of the beginning. The Last Gasp. The Big Kahuna. Computers will crash, to say nothing of passenger airplanes and the stock market. It'll be chaos, Phil. Sheer chaos. I'm getting out while I can. Would you like to buy my house?"

"How much?" I asked.

"You fill my camper with canned goods," said Matt, "and you've got yourself a deal."

"Wait a minute, Matt. I want to know what *else* it says in 2 Peter."

But Matt was gone. The phone line was a dull hum.

I decided to check out 2 Peter for myself then. That's when I found the rest of the story. The verses Matt missed.

Since everything will be destroyed in this way, what kind of people ought you to be? You ought to live holy and godly lives as you look forward to the day of God and speed its coming. That day will bring about the destruction of the heavens by fire, and the elements will melt in the heat. But in keeping with his promise we are looking forward to a new heaven and a new earth, the home of righteousness. So then, dear friends, since you are looking forward to this, make every effort to be found spotless, blameless and at peace with him. (2 Peter 3:11–14, NIV)

I really hope, I thought to myself, *that when Christ returns, He will find me playing catch with my kids. Or kissing my wife. Or sipping Coke with a nonbeliever. May He never find me frightened and shut away, thinking about the end.*

I tried to call Matt then. But all I got was a recording: "We are sorry, the number you have dialed has been disconnected. To pay

Matt's phone bill, please enter your credit card number at the beep." So I grabbed my Bible, jumped in the car and headed on over to Matt's house. I had two options: Talk him out of his decision, or if that failed, I would take him shopping. And fill his camper with canned goods.

TWENTY-SEVEN

Why Methusaleh Lived So Long

"Children are a great comfort in your old age—
and they help you reach it faster too."
LIONEL KAUFFMAN

I have on my desk an actual letter from Mrs. Anne Farley of Portland, Oregon. It says, "Dear Mr. Callaway, I enjoyed meeting you at camp this summer and I enjoyed listening to you speak, but I could not help noticing when I read your book that you look a lot older in real life than you do in your picture. Also you are quite bald and your hair is turning gray. Why do you think some people age so fast?"

I'd like to take this opportunity to thank Mrs. Farley for reminding me that if life is a loaf of bread, I'm molding as fast as anyone. Perhaps I'll send her a fruitcake this Christmas—labeled "best before 1973."

My eldest son deserves one too. On the night of my thirty-fifth birthday—in an act I will remember as long as I have functioning brain cells—he asked me, "How old are you again?" When I told him, he cocked his head to one side and said, "Wow! You're half dead!"

I think I handled the situation with admirable self-control. Calmly tucking the child into bed, I aimed a kiss squarely at his forehead, then went to my study and removed him from the will.

A few years have passed and I must admit that I'm aging even more rapidly than my son predicted. You may know the feeling. One night you go to bed feeling like a teenager and the next day you stand in front of the mirror asking out loud, "Hey, who kidnapped my body? Who replaced it with this wrinkled one?" You pass young people on the street and think they see a lean, trim, twenty-one-year-old. In actual fact, they see a middle-aged man who could be having a midlife crisis the very next time he glances through a photo album. On such occasions, it is important to remind ourselves that there are good reasons we are maturing so quickly. In my case, there are three good reasons: Two boys and a girl.

· Yes, throughout history children have been responsible for aging their parents. Back in Biblical times it took longer. Methusaleh lived 969 years. But remember that his children had not heard of dating, placing earrings in their noses, or loud music.

Recently I came home from a tough day at the office to find that our house was moving. Twelve-year-old Stephen and his nine-year-old brother Jeffrey had replaced my Michael Card tape with something that sounded like some very angry people had gotten together with the expressed purpose of harming one another with jackhammers. Though I'm sure the tape contained actual words, this is what I heard:

<blockquote>
OYA BOOM BOOM OYA BOOM BOOM
WAHOO BOOM BOOM
(Turn up volume and repeat chorus)
</blockquote>

"Hey! That sounds like somebody strangling a bagpiper!" I yelled. "TURN IT DOWN!"

"BURN *WHAT* DOWN?" hollered Jeffrey.

In the kitchen, Ramona was peacefully preparing supper—thanks to industrial-strength ear plugs.

"Guys," I said, after the volume control had been returned to its rightful spot, "when I was a boy, I was told that this kind of music kills plants. Chickens stop laying eggs when they hear this stuff. People start world wars. Let's find something else to do. Like go outside and see if this tape will burn."

"We kinda like it," they said.

Another big reason I am aging rapidly is the fact that some of my friends have teenagers. "You think things are bad now?" they say, with a glassy stare, "You just wait." I can only imagine. Already my daughter is approaching puberty at speeds upward of 900 miles an hour and it is only a matter of time before fourteen-year-old boys show up on our doorstep asking for her hand in marriage. If I sound paranoid, please forgive me. I'll feel better once I install land mines in the front yard.

Last night Dad and Mom came to visit. The same Dad and Mom who once asked me to turn my "music" down. The boys were playing dcTalk loudly enough to annoy people on Mars (which, interestingly, is where this band originates), and I noticed big grins on my parents' faces. *Perhaps,* I thought, *the real joy of grandparenting is watching your children be tortured with the same instruments they used to torture you.* But as the evening wore on I came to a very different conclusion.

You see, Mom and Dad didn't seem to notice the music as much as they noticed the kids. They listened as Stephen read the lyrics to "I'm into Jesus." They held grandchildren on their knees, took an interest in their homework, and asked them about their day. Seventy-five years of living had taught them that life passes too quickly for us to spend it majoring on the minors. And so I've watched them hug teenagers who have more earrings than brain cells. I've seen them on their knees confidently asking God to accomplish as much for their grandchildren as He has for their kids.

I don't know about you, but I need to be reminded of these things every now and then. I need to be reminded that the same God who has been faithful to each generation isn't about to stop with this one. I need to remember that although parenting is sometimes a frightening responsibility, it is also a joyful privilege. In fact, I wouldn't trade my kids for a good night's sleep. A full head of hair. Or some healthy plants.

Now, I'd better go. It's time to revise the will. And order up some fruitcake.

Mother... please tell me this isn't you in these hideous bell bottoms

TWENTY-EIGHT

The Last Resort

"The word which God has written on the brow of every man is hope."
VICTOR HUGO, AUTHOR OF LES MISÉRABLES (1802–1885)

I don't know about you, but God rarely seems to answer my prayers.

When I was five years old, I prayed that God would make me rich. It did not happen. The buck stopped before it got to our house. One day I overheard Dad tell Mom, "Honey, we have enough money to last us the rest of our lives. Unless we live past Thursday." That was about the sum of things.

In fourth grade I prayed day and night for a whole week that Gloryanne Larue would fall for me as deeply as I had fallen for her. I prayed that she would turn her petite dimples my way. Flash me her toothful smile. It did not happen. On Valentine's Day 1971 I walked forward to sharpen my pencil and casually eased a shiny Canadian dime from my pocket onto Gloryanne's desk, knowing that although my magnetic personality was enough of a draw, this emblem of my love and affection would undoubtedly seal our relationship, binding us together for time and eternity.

I was wrong. Dead wrong.

She did not even thank me. Or look my way the rest of that year. Once following another unanswered prayer, I thought about that dime. And wanted it back. I wanted to frame it. A small yet sad reminder of the times God seems to plug His ears when I pray. I suppose I don't need the dime. There are other reminders.

Recently a friend of mine asked me to pray for her. Her daughter had been experiencing headaches for the last week or so and the family doctor couldn't come up with a satisfying explanation. She was worried. She had read all about headaches in a woman's magazine and she found herself lying awake nights imagining the worst for her daughter. I told her I would pray for them both. And I did. A few days later she sent me the following note:

Dear Phil,

    Thanks for praying.

    You really get things started when you pray!

    I now have three children with the chicken pox. One is on codeine-laced drugs. The other two are pestering each other. This morning I decided to make them a treat—some cinnamon buns. Two and a half hours later, we heard a BANG and a CLINK! The glass baking dish had shattered in the oven, causing the butter from the cinnamon buns to drip onto the element. Which started a fire. Which caused me to throw a full canister of flour into the oven. Which caused smoke to billow throughout the house and flour to spill all over my freshly washed kitchen floor.

    Do you have any idea what happens to flour once it hits a wet floor, Phil? While I was tiptoeing around the kitchen in sticky feet, the doorbell rang. It was a vacuum cleaner salesman.

    Thanks for praying, Phil.

    Would you mind stopping now? Please?

    Sincerely, Gertie

I laughed out loud when I read this. *Perhaps she has a point*, I thought. *Too often my prayers seem to hit the ceiling then come crashing down, sticking to the floor.* In school I prayed that God would make me a straight A student...and got C's and D's. I asked God to make me the world's best hockey player...and scored into my own net. I prayed for girls to chase me...and watched them run the other way.

Of course, I have since realized how poor I would be if God had given me everything I asked for. As Billy Graham's wife Ruth once said, "God has not always answered my prayers. If he had, I would have married the wrong man—several times." But just once I'd love to pick up the phone and hear God's gentle voice of reassurance. Instead I find myself holding my end of the line, wondering why I've been put on permanent hold.

There have been times when I'd love to play the leading role in one of those amazing missionary stories I listened to as a kid. Like the one where the thirteen angels with flaming swords surrounded the missionary's hut to keep the cannibals away. As it turned out, thirteen men in Detroit were praying for the missionary family that very night. I loved that story. I almost wore out our record player listening to it.

But it never seemed to be *my* story.

Until one dark night in August of 1996. A night when God took me completely by surprise. Listen to my journal entries.

Friday, August 2, 1996

I think we're nearing the end. Ramona is down to ninety pounds. She went for a walk this morning and people in this little town didn't recognize her. A few dozen specialists have registered contradictory opinions and recommended endless medication. Now I know how guinea pigs feel. Nothing works. I've quit asking why, Lord. I'd just like to know where to go from here.

A week later, in a last ditch effort, I packed up the family and drove to a condo on a lake. I called it "The Last Resort." The setting was perfect. Mountains in the distance. Beaches in the foreground. "Dear God," I prayed, "I don't know what else to do. Please help her recover here."

But the seizures continued.

At night after everyone was asleep I sat by the water watching the last rays of sunlight paint the mountain peaks in dazzling pastels. On Wednesday, August 14, I took my journal with me and scrawled these words:

The children love it here. Stephen's been fishing (he's caught ten trout so far). Rachael's been spoiling the neighbor's toddlers. Jeffrey paddled around in a rubber raft most of today. I came up with a rather ingenious idea (ingenious for me!) which allowed me to stay by Ramona's side while watching him float. I tied one end of a rope to the raft and the other to a post on shore. Whenever he wanted to come in, he just pulled on the rope until he got here. Just after lunch I was praying prayers of desperation on the beach when a thought hit me (don't have too many of these...so need to pay attention!): When Jeffrey pulls himself in, he isn't pulling the shore to him. He's pulling himself to the shore. Maybe all this time I've been trying to pull God to my way of thinking—an impossible task—rather than lining up my desires with His. It took a while for this to sink in. But today I gave God the rope. I prayed, "Whatever you want, Lord. I'm yours." The sky did not look bluer. The water did not look clearer. But deep down I knew that I had been changed. That no matter what, all will be well.

We returned home a few days later. Ramona continued to deteriorate. One day a friend visited, only to discover that Ramona was having seizures every few hours. We prayed together, the three of us, and that night, after Ramona finally drifted off to sleep, I reclined on a lawn chair in our backyard looking up at the sky, tears staining my face.

"Dear God," I said out loud, "is there any hope? Or do I need to start making funeral arrangements?" Pushing myself from the chair, I fell to my knees pounding my fists on the ground. "God," I cried, "I can't take it anymore. Please do something."

The stars did not blink in unison. I saw no handwriting across the sky. But as I stood to my feet, a doctor's name came to mind. We attended the same church, but I'd never thought to ask his opinion. A few minutes later I had him on the phone. After listening to my description, he simply said: "I've seen this once before, Phil. It sounds like she has a rare chemical deficiency. Bring her to me first thing in the morning. There's a relatively new drug to treat it. It's called Epival."

I don't think I really believed in the power of prayer before that point in my life. But within a week, Ramona was a different person. The seizures ended. Her eyes lit up with the sparkle that first attracted me to her.

God had given me my wife back.

We're not through the valley. There are more tests ahead. But every day Ramona wakes up beside the most thankful guy in the world.

I'm thankful that God doesn't give us everything we want.

He gives us everything we need.

A few weeks after my backyard experience I wrote the following words in my journal:

August 28, 1996 (Our fourteenth anniversary)
It's been four years since our Les Misérables *weekend. Thanks, God, for getting us through. I told You today that I would do my best to start each day with You. Every morning when I wake up, I want to develop the habit of talking with You even before I kiss my wife. For too long You've been my last resort. I want You to be first in every situation. It seems that*

prayer is more about Your will than my desires. More about surrender than success. For years prayer has been my spare tire. Help it to be my steering wheel. When my knees knock, help me kneel on them. Even when everything is going well, I hope You'll find me there too. If prayer changes nothing else, let it change me.

If I were asked to pick out one single word that got us through almost five years of skunkbusting, it would be the glorious word "hope." Not just the hope that God would answer our prayers, but the hope that if He did not answer them the way we wanted, it was not the end of the story.

I learned this from many sources. From living in the psalms. From reading of the saints. But perhaps no one brought it closer to home than the hero of our next chapter. My friend Bruce.

SKUNKBUSTERS

Here are some actual prayers children have written to God:

Dear God,

Do you get your angels to do all the work? Mommy says we are her angels, and we have to do everything.

Love, Maria

Dear God,

Please put another holiday between Christmas and Easter. There is nothing good in there now.

Mike

Dear God,
When you started the earth and put people there and all the animals and grass and the stars, did you get very tired? I have a lot of other questions too.

Very truly yours, Sherman

Dear God,
Maybe Cain and Abel would not kill each other so much if they had their own rooms. It worked with my brother.

Love, Sharon

Dear God,
I am not selfish, but please let me grow. I'm too small. If you do, I'll be nice to my brother.

Suzanne, age 6

Dear God,
My grandpa has been gone since I was three. How is he doing?

Love, Rebecca, age 8

Dear God,
Why is the grass green? How did you make the clouds? What do you eat?

Danny, age 4

Dear God,
I think about you sometimes even when I'm not praying.

Love, Chester

•

During the Civil War, an anonymous Confederate soldier wrote:
I asked God for strength, that I might achieve;
I was made weak, that I may learn humbly to obey.
I asked God for health, that I may do greater things;
I was given infirmity, that I might do better things.
I asked for riches, that I may be happy;
I was given poverty, that I might be wise.
I asked for power, that I might have the praise of men;
I was given weakness, that I might feel the need of God.
I asked for all things, that I might enjoy life;
I was given life, that I might enjoy all things.
I got nothing I asked for but everything I hoped for.
I am, among all men, most richly blessed.

•

"My mother had a great deal of trouble with me,
but I think she enjoyed it."
MARK TWAIN

•

Motto of a Skunkbuster

I will view each obstacle as an opportunity
to draw closer to God.
I will let prayer change me
and deliver me from worry and fear.
I will value contentment over success,
joy over happiness,
compassion for others
over comfort for myself.
I will view each day as a chance
to live for Christ down here.
Knowing that a lifestyle of laughter
is possible for one reason only:
the end is a festival, not a funeral;
a resurrection, not a burial.

TWENTY-NINE

Hope for Christmas

"As long as matters are really hopeful,
hope is a mere flattery or platitude; it is when everything is hopeless
that hope begins to be a strength."
G. K. CHESTERTON

I t is Saturday morning. Outside the restaurant broad fluffy snowflakes are quietly burying memories of fall. Christmas is around the next corner. Near me parents and children are munching happily, storing energy so they don't drop when they shop. Across the table sits my friend Bruce. Something about him causes small children to stop and stare and parents to hustle them on by. But Bruce doesn't seem to mind. As he talks, I find myself wishing that everyone on earth would stop shopping long enough to listen to his captivating story.

Twenty Christmases ago, Bruce was staring out an apartment window, clutching a black leather Bible. Four floors below him frenzied shoppers bustled about searching for last minute gifts. As he wrestled again with what he was about to do, images of his life mingled with the shoppers: Running free along the forest trails…a small logging community…loving parents…good friends. Bruce smiled briefly as he thought of Sunday school. An ancient religion that never seemed to take hold. The smile quickly faded as he thought about that day in eighth grade. A day that changed everything. "Your father…dead…killed in a logging accident." He still could not erase the power of those words. They spelled the end of childhood. The beginning of a slippery descent.

Like the prodigal son, Bruce soon moved to the city to try life on his own. But he fared no better. Reform school was his first stop. Regular school was confining enough, but there was no recess here. On the other hand, he did pick up some useful trades. Pickpocketing 101. Advanced Break and Entry.

Graduation from reform school marked the beginning of a string of arrests and imprisonments. "One day I walked into a department store and took a hat off one dummy's head," grins Bruce, "placed it another dummy's head—mine—and walked out of the store." Minutes later he was arrested.

"'You keep going down this road,' a judge warned me a few months later, 'and you'll hit a dead end.' I knew it was time to change."

Before long Bruce found a job and upgraded his education. But soon the old lifestyle beckoned. "I was more qualified to steal than work," he admits. "Besides, what did it matter? Every time I tried schooling or honest work I only found more trouble…or prison time."

A waitress offers us menus, but Bruce declines. "Just a Coke, please," I say. I can tell he's having trouble breathing. "You okay?" I ask. He's okay. As the waitress pours, the story continues.

Just before Christmas, the long nights of winter moved in, encircling him with their cold clammy talons. Defeat and an overwhelming sense of failure took over his life. Hope was fading fast. A new job held promise. Until a boss learned he'd done time. His live-in girlfriend of four years walked out the door, leaving him alone. He couldn't remember quietness ever sounding so loud.

As a child the Christmas season had been a time for laughter. For parties and friends, short walks and long toasts. But not this Christmas. From the fourth story window, Bruce studied the cold, lifeless pavement below and thought of his life. The depression would never lift. His hopes, once dim possibilities, now only taunted him. The bleak winter mirrored a despair so deep that there was only one way out.

Gripping the spine of the Bible, he hurled it across the room and watched it bounce off the wall. Then he walked resolutely toward the fridge, turned around, and raced toward the open window.

ॐ

He awoke, straining his eyes to look up. Above him was a stuccoed hospital ceiling. "I couldn't believe it," he says now. "My arms were broken, I had a ruptured spleen, shredded knees, and a broken jaw. I swore at myself. All I could think of was, 'Gee Bruce, you're such a failure you can't even kill yourself.'"

Wheeling himself numbly down the hall one day, he met an old friend. "Listen," said the friend, after they exchanged greetings, "you need to talk to a lady I know. Here's her phone number."

Bruce looked at the name. And remembered. Ten years ago this lady had tried to cram religion down his throat. It hadn't worked. Politely he put the number in his wallet and forgot about it.

Back on the streets, he found himself walking a familiar path. A downward slope. Old memories began to haunt him. Old feelings returned. One day he reached into his wallet and dialed the number. This time he was ready to listen.

They talked for hours. "Bruce," the lady told him, "God loves you so much that He sent His only Son to die for your sins. It doesn't matter what you've done, He will accept you. He's the only religious leader who doesn't have a grave marker on His tomb, Bruce. And He loves to turn things around. Give people a new start. A new life. Purpose and peace."

Alone in his kitchen that night, Bruce elbowed aside some dishes and folded his hands. "Jesus," he prayed, tears inching down his face, "I don't know what you'd want with a guy like me. But if you can make something good of this mess...here I am...I need you...I need you bad."

Some changes came easily, others were slow. Bruce shook his head when he realized how much he loved reading the Bible he'd thrown against the wall. *It's solid,* he thought. *Unbreakable.* Church became his new hangout and through the guidance of friends there, things began to change. He completed a nurse's aide program and found work.

In September of 1986, the government granted him a full pardon.

"I've always believed it was a direct result of first being pardoned by the blood of Christ," Bruce says. "And right away I realized I'd like nothing more than to go back to jail. This time I'd like to be chaplain."

In a cafeteria line one day, he caught the eye of a pretty young maiden from Michigan. He had no idea that Suzy was a widow. Or that she had three young children and a silver Yorkshire terrier named Morgan. "At forty, I couldn't imagine myself married, much less the father of three," he says.

Suzy wasn't ready either. "It takes many years to train a man right," she jokes. "I didn't know if I wanted to start again!"

On July 15, 1989, they were married. Together with three children and a very furry dog, they traveled from Michigan to Victoria, Canada, spending the nights in a four-man tent. Bruce laughs when he tells me about it. "Someone told me that the shortest sentence in the English language is 'I am.' And the longest is 'I do.' But marriage has been marvelous. Not perfect. Just the second best thing that ever happened to me."

He memorized a verse. One that seemed appropriate: "In all things God works for the good of those who love him" (Romans 8:28, NIV). How true it was. His new family would watch him graduate from seminary soon. A life once filled with despair now held all the promise in the world.

Bruce smiles as he remembers those days. He looks out the window. The snowflakes seem larger than ever. The smile fades. A storm is on its way.

Four months after graduation, Bruce sat in a stuffy doctor's office feeling like he had back in eighth grade. He could only stare in disbelief. The words were distant, impossible.

"You have cancer, Bruce. It's terminal."

The doctor cleared his throat.

"Mesothelioma has never been successfully treated. I'm sorry. You have four months to live. Nine if things go well."

It wasn't the first time Bruce had stared death in the face. Pain loomed on the horizon. Hopes of a chaplaincy were shattered. "I remember thinking, *I will never watch my kids graduate or marry. I will never hold a grandchild.*"

When he broke the news to the kids, there was stunned silence. Finally Erin, the youngest, blurted out, "This is my second dad. It's not fair!"

"She was right," says Bruce. "I guess there's nothing more challenging than trusting God when everything inside me cries out against what's happening."

A few days after the diagnosis Bruce visited me in my office. "I had all these hopes…" he began, staring at a bookcase above my head. "Hopes to be a chaplain…hopes to make a difference in this world…I had all these hopes…" Then a smile came to his face. And he chuckled. "I guess all I've got now is *hope!*"

As the weeks turned to months Bruce began the job of reconciliation. He'd inflicted many wounds in his prison years, so he searched phone books and asked forgiveness. For the first time family members began to listen as he told them about Jesus. And he decided he might as well work towards being a prison chaplain anyway.

Prison authorities loved the mild-mannered preacher. Until he came equipped with an oxygen tank. If he were taken hostage, one said, it could be used as a bomb. No problem, said the others. Bruce is different. We'll work with it.

One day while sitting in church a few rows ahead of me, one of Bruce's oxygen tubes sprung a leak. It sounded like he was about to deflate. People didn't know what to do. Before fixing the problem Bruce turned around with a "Help, I'm about to explode," expression on his face. We all laughed. And felt better.

As I finish my Coke, a small child stops before our table. "What's that, Mister?" he says, staring at the tubes and oxygen tank.

I can overhear his dad: "Come on…don't stare…keep moving."

But Bruce leans over and offers part of the tube to the child. The boy holds it in his fingers, feeling the air pulse through.

"It's oxygen," says Bruce. "It keeps me alive."

The little boy smiles widely and looks up at his dad. "Can I have one too?" he asks.

During a trip to St. Lucia, a few people stopped to ask Bruce why he didn't like to breathe their air. Bruce laughed. And told them about cancer. And where he was going when he breathed his last.

Back home Bruce continued to outlive the doctors' most optimistic predictions. He seemed to live life with purpose, taking special delight in praying with inmates, and helping children who weren't learning as quickly as their parents wanted them to. When he entered a classroom, kids followed him like the Pied Piper. "Hey, it's the guy with the mask!" they said. For the Olympics, Bruce erected a large Canadian flag and cheered wildly. He borrowed movies from me. Adventure movies. Comedy classics. His family fought over his favorite chair, a reclining green rocker, worn by the years. But when Bruce was home, it was his. "It's the best seat in the house," he said. And Morgan thought so too.

"Do you ever get discouraged, Bruce?" I ask, as I finish yet another Coke. "Do you ever get down?"

"Oh yes," he replies. "But I keep a prayer book. I have notes, pictures, prayer requests in it. I take it everywhere, and when I'm discouraged I open it up and write something to others or pray for them. There are plenty of people worse off than me. Think of it—Michael Jackson pays money to sleep in an oxygen tent! Insurance pays for mine. Besides, this thing will run out one day. And I'll be Home."

"Do you ever ask why God allowed this to happen?"

"Sometimes. But I've had peace you can't explain. Friends who really care. I've lived four years longer than I should have. So I wake up each morning realizing that the tomorrow I wasn't supposed to have is here today. Each day is a bonus. I've lived long enough to watch my children graduate. I've given one away in marriage. And I had the privilege of baptizing Erin a few summers ago. I have time to do the stuff that really matters now. I'm blessed, I really am. I think it's helped to keep a sense of humor about myself and my circumstances. There's no stronger medication than a good chuckle. But I must admit that I'm tired now. Heaven is getting more appealing every day."

On December 27, two days after Christmas, Bruce fell asleep in his favorite green chair. And awoke in heaven.

Sitting near me at the funeral was a young woman Bruce had led to the foot of the Cross. The service was videotaped for the inmates at his favorite penitentiary. And Bruce had planned the service, right down to the words inscribed on the front of the bulletin.

Words written in prison by the president of the Czech Republic, Vaclav Havel:

> Hope is definitely not the same thing as optimism.
> It is not the conviction that something will turn out well.
> But the certainty that something makes sense.
> Regardless of how it turns out.

I will miss my friend. If you knew Bruce you'd understand why. His life emanated hope. His face radiated joy. Bruce was the kind of guy who left even the undertaker feeling sorry when he died.

I dreamed of Bruce one night. He was in heaven surrounded by family and friends, by inmates and small children. The oxygen tank was gone, but he was sitting on his favorite recliner laughing about the bad old days.

"Great to see you," he said. "Join us...I've got the best seat in the house."

THIRTY

A Place Called Home

"Turn up the lights, I don't want to go home in the dark."
THE LAST WORDS OF O. HENRY

Today on my way home from work
    I passed a dozen houses.
It's one of the joys of a small town, this walk home.
I love a place where people honk
    only to say hi.
Some of the houses I pass are dilapidated,
    others groomed to perfection.
The millionaire's place on the corner is framed in brick,
    its expansive yard causes heads to turn.
But today I didn't notice.
Today when I took a left through a field of dandelions
    and saw the cappacino-colored cottage

nestled near the railway tracks,
             my pace quickened.
Today I realized for the very first time
      that I pick up speed—
             the closer I get
                   to home.
I suppose I've always wanted a place of my own.
      A backyard pool.
                   An underground gym.
      Maybe a tennis court or two.
But I settled for three bedrooms.
      Three children.
                   And one wife.
A few years from now we'll have three teenagers.
      We'll add another room.
                   We'll need more prayer.
Last week we celebrated 18 months here.
      It finally feels like home, said Ramona.
                   I think it's the memories.
Saturday night pizza.
      Midwinter barbecues.
                   Kids jumping on us early Christmas morning.
Midnight conversations.
      Barefoot walks.
      Arguments, too.
Stephen's guppies,
      Rachael's dolls,
                   Jeffrey's laugh.
                         Ah, how I love this place we call home.
But I've noticed something else lately.
      A month ago a toilet seal gave way.
                   Guess who fixed it?
Spring showed up a leaky basement.
      It's on my list.

So is a dripping tap,
a frayed carpet,
a pantry door that's been a real
pane.

What we construct eventually corrodes.
Sidewalks crack.
Paint peels.
Houses decay.

We're constantly rebuilding.
Renovating.
Restoring the stuff of earth.

Don't get me wrong.
I love it here.
I love rooms dancing with memories.
Halls loud with laughter.
Even sticky fingerprints on windows.

But leaky toilets and wet basements have a way of reminding
us that
nothing lasts forever.
Nothing here.
That this house is a poor substitute for
Home.

Tonight the television shows visions of a far-off war.
Of a high school massacre closer to home.
A judge calls child porn acceptable,
wouldn't want to trample anyone's freedom of choice.
My Blue Jays lost a nail-biter.
The weather report looks daunting.
Dark tonight. Darker tomorrow.
It's harder and harder to call this place
home.

Home sounds more like a place where pain is a distant memory.
Where God makes everything new.

Where wheelchairs and tears are noticeably absent.
Home sounds like a place where joy and laughter are permanent.

> Where God's people touch nail scars,
>> bow in awe. And celebrate an empty tomb.

My son says I'm aging fast.
Picking up speed the closer I get to Home.

>> Tonight, for the very first time, I don't really mind.

The hope of Home gives me purpose here.

> To live each day like it's a bonus.
>> To take God's hand and walk bravely into tomorrow.
>> Passing grace along.

At times I wish I had answers

> for the pain
>> for the suffering.

But for now it's enough to know that one day soon—

> I will be Home.
> For good.

That one day soon my questions will be straightened—

> into exclamation points.

That those arms that spread wide on a Roman cross,

> will open once again.
> Inviting me in.

To a place God Himself took a few thousand years to build.
A place called Home.

Epilogue

The encyclopedia tells me that one skunk can be found for every ten acres of land. We live on the edge of a ten-acre town. Guess where the skunk lives?

One summer night, during the very week I began writing this book, I was awakened at 2 A.M. by a motion sensor light on our back deck. Few people lock their doors around here, and one's mind does not immediately go to burglars. Instead I lay there wondering if my neighbor Vance had come to borrow something from my fridge (this has happened before), or if he was searching for my car keys because he's out of gas (this has happened too). I rose quickly from my bed, donned a green housecoat, and pulled aside a blind.

Nothing.

No movement.

Not a sound.

The previous night I'd been awakened by a committee meeting of cats who couldn't agree on much, but tonight I could find no intruder. Suddenly our garbage can moved. Sure enough. A black cat was halfway inside, up to its hips in potato peels. I opened the door and stepped outside.

"Psssst," I hissed. "Get outta here."

The cat moved not a whisker.

"HEY YOU," I yelled, "SCRAM!" My wife sat up straight as an arrow, as if Gabriel had just blown the last trumpet.

Picking up a Sunday shoe, I hurled it at the garbage can. The shoe missed. The cat didn't move. Then I noticed several things at once. For a cat, this customer was rather cool. Then I saw a white stripe down its back. And smelled a pungent odor. One which reminded me of that summer evening so many pages ago when Bobby and I lifted the lid on the old Ford Fairlane and closed the shades on the Finney family vacation.

Standing in my housecoat at 2 A.M., I smiled at the memories, briefly considered laying down a trail of lettuce to Vance's house, then quickly retreated inside.

During breakfast the next morning, one of the children almost choked on his porridge. "Lookit!" Jeffrey yelled. Sure enough, the skunk's trail had taken him across the railway tracks and into a small hole two hundred feet from our back door. The kids could scarcely contain their excitement. Imagine, sharing your address with a skunk!

"Let's tame him, Dad," they said. "Get him de-skunked." I had other solutions in mind. But the kids took a liking to the skunk. Named him Samson. Samson Callaway. Believe me, when the west wind blows, he's the strongest creature in town.

As fall became winter, the smell subsided and the skunk seemed to disappear. I wondered what happened to Samson, but instead of checking the cave across the tracks, I pulled out the encyclopedia. These critters don't really hibernate, it said. They just slow down.

I suppose it's the same in life. Sometimes the skunk lurks at our back door. At other times it seems to disappear altogether, giving us time to breathe again. But there are few guarantees down here.

Not long ago, as spring winds rose in the west, pushing clouds from the mountains, I noticed a familiar scent. Samson was stirring again. I sniffed the air. And smiled. For the first time in nine months I didn't feel like killing the little critter. Perhaps I'll leave him there, I thought. After all, I could use an occasional reminder to practice what I've been preaching throughout this book. A reminder that a little laughter goes a long way when it comes to attitude. That fear is okay if it drives us to our knees. That the strongest roots grow best in the dark. And that in the toughest of times, we have more than we think…when we have hope.

A few days before putting the finishing touches on the final chapter of this book, I received a letter from a long-distance friend by the name of Ron. Ron is a five-star skunkbuster. His letter told of the birth of his newborn daughter Faith Nicole. He described her tiny fingers, her deep blue eyes, her wavy brown hair, and her enthusiastic cry. Then he told of the disappointment of a doctor's diagnosis. Of holding Faith in his arms one last time. Of her last breath. Of her journey Home.

Then, in true "skunkbuster" fashion, this father penned some inspiring words: "We are very grateful for the time we were given and the memories made during those few short hours. We have rolls of film to help us remember this wonderful gift of God. Our hearts are broken, yet we rejoice in the hope that is ours in Christ Jesus. Even in the midst of our hurt, we are able to see God's gracious mercy. We asked for strength to face the difficulties of this pregnancy and birth, and God came alongside in the form of friends and family. We asked for a healthy child. Faith is healthy and whole...in heaven. We asked for acceptance of God's will no matter what the outcome, and that too is happening...one moment at a time."

Ron doesn't have all the answers yet. But he's beginning to recognize that while Faith is gone, his faith has never been stronger. He concludes his letter with two five-star verses from 2 Corinthians:

> For our present troubles are quite small and won't last very long. Yet they produce for us an immeasurably great glory that will last forever! So we don't look at the troubles we can see right now, rather we look forward to what we have not yet seen. For the troubles we see will soon be over, but the joys to come will last forever. (2 Corinthians 4:17–18)

Perhaps you've been sharing an address with a skunk lately. Or maybe the scent is gone for now. Either way, I pray that you'll hang onto those verses. And I pray that this book has renewed in you the same sense of hope that Ron has. A hope that makes all the difference in how we respond to the skunks of life.

Now, I'd better go. It's late. And the back light is on. Perhaps it's my neighbor Vance. Or a cat. Or it could be the strongest creature in town.

Phil would love to hear your "skunk" story. Write him at:
Phil Callaway
P.O. Box 4576
Three Hills, AB TOM 2NO
E-mail: phil.callaway@pbi.ab.ca

Phil is editor of *Servant* magazine, an award-winning magazine read in 101 countries. A ministry of Prairie Bible Institute, *Servant* is full of insightful interviews with well-known Christians, helpful articles, world news, and Phil's trademark humor. For a complimentary one-year subscription, please call 1-800-221-8532, or write:

Servant Magazine
Box 4000
Three Hills, AB Canada
TOM 2NO

About the Author

Phil Callaway is an award-winning columnist and a popular speaker at conferences, churches, and camps. The author of *Making Life Rich without Any Money, Honey I Dunked the Kids,* and *Daddy I Blew Up the Shed,* Phil's writings have been translated into languages like Spanish, Polish, Chinese, and English—one of which he speaks fluently. His five-part video series, *The Big Picture,* has been circulated in thousands of churches worldwide. Phil is married to his high school sweetheart Ramona, and lives in Alberta, Canada, with his three children (his wife lives there, too). Phil says he is one of only eight living people who has not seen the film *Titanic.* For more information on his books, videos, or speaking ministry, you may write P.O. Box 4576, Three Hills, AB TOM 2NO, 403-443-8028.